# PERSPECTIVES ON PSYCHOLOGY

# PERSPECTIVES ON PSYCHOLOGY

## MICHAEL W. EYSENCK

**A volume in the series**
*Principles of Psychology*

*Series Editors*
Michael W. Eysenck
Simon Green
Nicky Hayes

LAWRENCE ERLBAUM ASSOCIATES, PUBLISHERS
Hove (UK)                    Hillsdale (USA)

Reprinted in paperback 1995

Lawrence Erlbaum Associates Ltd., Publishers
27 Palmeira Mansions
Church Road
Hove
East Sussex, BN3 2FA
UK

**British Library Cataloguing in Publication Data**

A catalogue record for this book is available from the British Library

ISBN 0-86377-254-4 (hbk)
ISBN 0-86377-255-2 (pbk)
ISSN 0965-9706

Cartoons by Sanz
Subject index compiled by Sue Ramsey
Cover design by Stuart Walden and Joyce Chester
Printed and bound by BPC Wheatons Ltd, Exeter, UK

*To my daughter, Juliet, with love*

# Preface

This book forms part of a series that is designed to provide detailed coverage of the major areas of psychology. All the books in the series have been written in such a way that they are readily understandable, even to those who have not previously studied psychology.

The focus of this book is on the nature of psychology, and on the different perspectives psychologists have adopted in their efforts to understand human and animal behaviour. There is a fair amount of coverage of the history of psychology, because it is easier to make sense of contemporary psychology when one has seen how psychology has evolved. There is also a chapter on the conduct of research, which examines some of the moral issues confronted by psychologists in the course of their research.

I am very grateful to my family for their support during the preparation of this book. The fact that I have recently completed four books for Lawrence Erlbaum Associates means I am in the fortunate position of being able to dedicate a book to my wife and to each of our three children! By the luck of the draw, this particular book is dedicated to our youngest child, Juliet.

# Contents

# Introduction 1

## What is psychology?

**A**useful starting point for this book is to consider what is meant by psychology. Most people have some idea what psychology is about, but they are often confused by the distinction between psychology and psychiatry. In fact, it is easier to define "psychiatry" than "psychology": psychiatry is concerned with the study and treatment of mental disorders, and psychiatrists have medical degrees. The definition of psychology has changed over the centuries, so it will be useful to adopt a historical approach.

## The background

The word "psychology" means different things to different people. It derives from the Greek words *psyche*, meaning mind or soul, and *logos*, meaning study. Therefore, at least at one time, psychology was regarded as the study of the mind.

For many centuries it was generally believed that human beings had minds, but no other species did. As a consequence, psychology was almost entirely concerned with the study of the human mind. The easiest and most obvious way of investigating the human mind is by means of *introspection* (defined in the *Oxford English Dictionary* as "examination or observation of one's own mental processes"), and we shall be looking at this in Chapter 3.

The greatest challenge to the view that psychology is the study of the mind came from Charles Darwin in the nineteenth century, with his theory of evolution (see Chapter 2). If the human species has evolved from other species, it is a little difficult (although not impossible) to see how we could have minds when these other species do not. So, as psychologists reacted to the Darwinian revolution, their views of the nature of psychology began to change.

In the early twentieth century, the *behaviourists* in America argued that neither humans nor any other species possessed minds. This argument obviously makes sense if we have evolved from species that don't have minds. However, if minds don't exist, this poses some problems for the

THE PSYCHOLOGICAL EVOLUTION OF MAN.

notion that psychology is the study of the mind! Instead, the behaviourists argued, psychology is (or should be) the science of behaviour.

As we will see in Chapter 2, the behaviourist revolution not only changed the emphasis of psychology from the study of the mind to the study of behaviour; it also altered the methods regarded as suitable for psychology. The emphasis began to shift from introspection to the *experimental method*, in which observations of behaviour were made under carefully controlled laboratory conditions. What is more, if psychology is the science of behaviour, there is no good reason for studying only humans. It is relatively straightforward to measure the behaviour of other species under controlled conditions, and evolution means that one might expect to find some important similarities across species.

## Current viewpoints

What is the contemporary view of the nature of psychology? Most textbooks still define psychology as the science of behaviour, but this doesn't mean psychologists agree with all the beliefs of behaviourists.

One of the differences is that most psychologists nowadays are willing to regard introspective reports of experience and thoughts as valid forms of behaviour, whereas the behaviourists were not. Another difference is that behaviourists tended to be interested in behaviour itself, but contemporary psychologists usually regard behaviour as of interest mainly because it sheds light on internal processes. In other words, behaviour is used to draw inferences about those internal processes.

We have seen how psychologists were initially concerned solely with the mind, and then more recently denied its existence altogether, so what is the current view of the mind's relevance to psychology? Many contemporary psychologists would subscribe to an "iceberg" theory of the mind, with the conscious mind corresponding to the visible tip of the iceberg. There is probably a natural human tendency to exaggerate the importance of the conscious mind, because we don't have direct access to the much larger non-conscious mind. However, a couple of examples will perhaps help to convince you that much human behaviour relies remarkably little on the conscious mind.

There are several different and complex skills involved in riding a bicycle, and yet most cyclists have almost no conscious awareness of any of the knowledge they possess about cycling. More strikingly, imagine running down a spiral staircase. If you started thinking about where to place each foot, you would greatly enhance the chances of ending up in a heap at the bottom of the stairs! In this case, use of the conscious mind would actually be disruptive rather than helpful.

There have clearly been substantial changes in psychologists' views of the nature of psychology over the centuries, although only some of the important ones have been mentioned. It is essential to realise that even current psychologists differ among themselves about the appropriate definition of psychology. The majority believe psychology should be based on the scientific study of behaviour, but that the conscious mind forms an important part of its subject matter. However, there are alternative contemporary views of the nature of psychology, and some of them are dealt with later in this book.

## "Psychology is just common sense"

One of the peculiar features of psychology is the way everyone is to a greater or lesser extent a psychologist. We all observe the behaviour of other people and ourselves, and everyone has access to their own conscious thoughts and feelings.

This "everyman" factor is relevant to us, because one of the tasks of psychologists is to predict behaviour, and the prediction of behaviour is important in everyday life. The better we are able to anticipate how other people will react in any given situation, the more contented and rewarding our social interactions are likely to be.

But the fact that everyone is a psychologist has led many sceptics to belittle the achievements of scientific psychology. This is often accomplished by putting professional psychologists in a "catch-22" situation, which some find rather irritating. If the findings of scientific psychology are in accord with common sense, the sceptic argues they tell us nothing we didn't know already. On the other hand, if the findings do not accord with common sense, the sceptic's reaction is, "I don't believe it!".

There are numerous deficiencies in the view that scientific psychology does not represent an advance on common sense, and we can look at two of the main ones. In the first place, it is misleading to assume that common sense forms a coherent set of assertions about behaviour. This can readily be seen if we regard proverbs as illustrative of commonsensical views. A girl parted from her lover may be saddened if she thinks of the proverb "Out of sight, out of mind", but she will presumably be cheered up if she tells herself that "Absence makes the heart grow fonder". There are several other pairs of proverbs which express opposite meanings—for example, "Look before you leap" can be contrasted with "He who hesitates is lost",

'LOOK BEFORE YOU LEAP' vs. 'HE WHO HESITATES IS LOST.'

and "Many hands make light work" is the opposite of "Too many cooks spoil the broth". As common sense involves such inconsistent views of human behaviour, it obviously can't be used as the basis for explaining that behaviour.

The notion that psychology is just common sense can also be refuted by considering psychological experiments in which the results were very different from those most people would have anticipated.

One of the most famous examples is the work of Stanley Milgram (1974). An experimenter divided his subjects into pairs to play the roles of teacher and pupil in a simple learning test. The teacher was asked to administer electric shocks to the pupil every time the wrong answer was given, and to increase the shock intensity each time. At 180 volts, the learner yelled "I can't stand the pain", and by 270 volts the response had become an agonised scream. If the "teacher" showed a reluctance to administer the shocks, the experimenter (a professor of psychology) urged him or her to continue.

Do you think you would be willing to administer the maximum (and potentially lethal) 450-volt shock in this experiment? What percentage of other people do you think would be prepared to do it? Milgram discovered that everyone denied that they personally would do any such thing; and psychiatrists at a leading medical school predicted only one person in a thousand would go on to the 450-volt stage. In fact, approximately 50% of Milgram's subjects gave the maximum shock—which is 500 times as many people as the expert psychiatrists had predicted! In other words, people are more conformist and obedient to authority than they realise. More specifically, there is a strong tendency to go along with the decisions of someone (such as a professor of psychology) who is apparently a competent authority figure. (In case you are wondering about the fate of the unfortunate "learner" in this experimental situation, it should be pointed out that he was a "stooge" and didn't actually receive any shocks at all.)

In sum, we can see common sense isn't much use in understanding and predicting human behaviour. According to most psychologists, the best way of achieving these goals is to investigate behaviour under controlled conditions, by means of the experimental and other methods available to the psychological researcher. These methods are discussed in detail in Chapter 5.

# The beginnings of psychology

The history of psychology spans a period of over 2000 years, from the ancient Greeks through to the present day. Most of the advances in psychology have happened over the past 150 years or so, but it is well worth having a brief look at some of the earlier theoretical contributions of the great philosophers and thinkers. Their views are of interest in themselves, and also provide a context within which later theory and research can be understood more readily.

## Ancient Greeks

Intellectual activity flourished astonishingly in ancient Greece in the fifth and fourth centuries BC. Before that time, nearly all thinking had been either severely practical or devoted to the world of the imagination; but Socrates, Plato, Aristotle, and others introduced an abstract, critical way of thinking about people and the world. This new thinking was known as *philosophy*—seeking after wisdom or knowledge. The key characteristics of their approach involved a sceptical questioning of conventional beliefs.

Socrates, who lived between 470 and 399 BC, was an influential philosopher whose ideas have come down to us largely through the writings of his pupil Plato (427–347 BC). In turn, Aristotle (384–322 BC) became the pupil of Plato, and for a while was also the tutor of Alexander the Great. Although Socrates influenced Plato, and Plato influenced Aristotle, there were nevertheless major intellectual differences among them, especially between Plato and Aristotle.

Plato argued for a sharp distinction between the body and the soul. According to him, science was nothing but "a game and a recreation"; it was a "presumptious prying of man into the divine order of nature". The evidence of one's senses provided unreliable information; true knowledge could be attained only through thought.

In spite of Plato's scepticism about the value of science, he nevertheless had much to say that is relevant to psychology. For example, he made it clear in his writings that he believed in the importance of individual differences, and that such differences could have their basis in what was inherited. He compared memory with fixing impressions in wax, and suggested that individuals differ in the receptivity of "the wax in their souls". In his political writings, he compared different groups in society with different metals, with one group being likened to gold, another to silver, and a third to iron and copper. The metal of which they were formed determined their standing in society. Plato also played a major role in developing the notion of "mental health", and believed the body and the mind were both important factors. The body needed gymnastic training, whereas the mind needed a training of the emotions through the arts, and of the intellect through mathematics, philosophy, and science.

It is well known that Plato distinguished between the soul and the body, but less so that he developed a reasonably complex hierarchical theory of the soul. In essence, he argued that the soul is simply the principle of life at its lowest level, whereas the emotions are at the intermediate or desiring level. Finally, at the top level, there is the rational and intelligent part of the mind, which has the least connection with the body. There are tantalising similarities between this theory of the soul and Freud's division of the mind into the id (seat of motivational instincts), ego (rational mind), and superego (conscience).

In contrast to Plato, Aristotle argued that there was a close relationship between the body and the soul. The soul, or "psyche", was defined simply as the functioning of the active processes of the body: "It is better not to speak of the soul as feeling pity or as learning or thinking, but rather the man as doing this through the soul". The logic of Aristotle's position is that psychology should be regarded as an extension of biology—a view that is still perfectly reasonable today.

Aristotle thought scientific research was of great value in under-standing human behaviour. Indeed, there are grounds for claiming that he was the first systematic scientific researcher. He believed science should proceed by making observations to establish the facts, and should then attempt to provide an explanation of those facts. Aristotle's views on the proper relationship between theory and observation have a very modern ring about them. Consider, for example, this quotation from his discussion of animal movement: "And we must grasp this not only gener-ally in theory, but also by reference to individuals in the world of sense, for with these in view we seek general theories, and with these we believe that general theories ought to harmonise".

The popular view of Aristotle is primarily of a philosopher and a logician. However, we've already seen that he was also interested in science, and he did in fact make numerous significant contributions in this field. For example, he studied the development of the embryos in hens' eggs, which were opened at various points during incubation, and his observations made him the founder of embryology. It is particularly relevant to note his strong claims as the first psychologist, in the sense of someone committed to using theory and research to understand human behaviour. Whether or not these claims are accepted, it is indisputable that Aristotle devoted much of his attention to psychological issues.

One of the problems with evaluating Aristotle's views on psychology is that, for the most part, we have a large collection of lecture notes rather than his own written works. Nevertheless, we do know he believed that some important differences between individuals are produced by hered-ity, whereas others stem from habitual patterns of responding which are established early in life. This acknowledgement of the combined influ-ences of heredity and environment on individual differences in behaviour is very much in line with contemporary thinking (see Chapter 3).

Aristotle's views on emotion also have a contemporary feel. He proposed that emotions have three essential components: the first is associated with the body; the second is the experience of pleasure or pain; and the third is based on thought (e.g. fear is "due to a mental picture of some destructive or painful evil in the future").

Probably the best-known of Aristotle's psychological theories is the idea that people, events, and things tend to be linked and remembered on the basis of three *laws of association*: contiguity or closeness; similarity; and contrast. For example, seeing Jane can make us think of Peter because we've previously seen Jane and Peter together (law of contiguity); or because Jane and Peter resemble each other (law of similarity); or because they're very different from each other (law of contrast).

To be fair to Plato, he had previously argued for the importance of contiguity and similarity. However, Aristotle developed and extended Plato's ideas, and provided the first recorded example of a chain association: "milk, white, mist, moist, autumn".

It is difficult to capture the essence of Aristotle's enormous contribution to psychology. Nevertheless, it can safely be said that he had a very sophisticated view of the scientific method, and of the proper relationship between experimental findings and theoretical models. The crucial significance of his contribution can be seen in this quotation from Charles Darwin, who was himself one of the most influential figures in the history of psychology: "Linnaeus and Cuvier have been my two gods, but they were mere schoolboys to old Aristotle". What is perhaps the greatest compliment to Aristotle's eminence, however, is the fact that, for almost 2000 years after his death, psychology didn't advance significantly beyond the position he had reached.

## The seventeenth century

For reasons that are probably best left to historians to explain, psychology (and most other sciences) went into relative decline for several centuries after the intellectual flourishing of Ancient Greece. This decline was halted and reversed by a number of outstanding scientists in the sixteenth and seventeenth centuries. In the mid-sixteenth century, Copernicus argued that the earth and the planets moved around the sun; Galileo investigated issues such as gravity and the laws governing pendulum movements; and Sir Isaac Newton revolutionised great areas of scientific knowledge.

Psychology was relatively slow to respond to the exciting intellectual atmosphere of the times, perhaps because of its comparative complexity. It is especially perplexing that the seventeenth-century approach to psychology was almost totally devoid of any attempts to conduct proper experiments, in great contrast to the approach taken by scientists such as

Galileo and Sir Isaac Newton. Presumably it was believed experiments would be unable to shed any real light on the mind or soul, and so were of very limited potential value.

René Descartes (1596–1650) was the first major figure in seventeenth-century psychology. He claimed that animals resemble machines, in that their actions are predictable from physical laws. (This mechanistic approach to animal psychology is broadly consistent with the theoretical stance adopted by the behaviourists in the early years of the twentieth century.) But only part of human behaviour could be explained in the mechanistic terms applicable to animals. Human thought and rational decision-making illustrated the workings of the soul or mind, by which Descartes basically meant consciousness.

These views produced a very real problem. If the body and the soul are radically different from each other, how is it they can influence one another? Descartes came up with the bold (but unfortunately wrong) answer that the place where the body and soul interact is the pineal gland, which is located within the brain. Most features of the brain are duplicated in both hemispheres, but there is only one pineal gland. As there is only one soul, this made the pineal gland the favoured location of the soul. But, apart from the dubious choice of the pineal gland as its seat, it was not at all clear how something as lacking in physical form as the soul could influence a physical structure such as the pineal gland.

Descartes had an enormous influence over a long period of time. However, there are grounds for agreeing with Hearnshaw (1987) that he mainly succeeded in directing psychology down a cul-de-sac. Descartes argued that the most important part of a human being (i.e. the mind or soul) had no biological reality, and could not be studied by the methods of science. Such a viewpoint clearly implied that proper scientific psychology was not possible.

Another limitation of Descartes' views stemmed from his identification of the mind with consciousness. This identification denied the possibility of mental processes occurring below the level of conscious awareness; and perhaps helps explain the marked reluctance of many psychologists to accept the strong evidence for unconscious mental processes.

Gottfried Leibnitz (1646–1716) in Germany was also occupied with the issue of the relationship between the soul and the body, or between mental and physical processes. He agreed with Descartes that the mind and the body are very different, but he rejected Descartes' view that they interact with each other.

Leibnitz proposed instead a doctrine known as *psychophysical parallelism*. According to this theory, God established a harmony at the beginning of the universe so that mental and physical events occur simultaneously, like two synchronised clocks or orchestras. As a consequence of this "pre-established harmony", it seems as if the mind and the body interact. In fact, Leibnitz argued, mental processes are affected only by preceding mental processes, and physical processes by earlier physical processes.

Psychophysical parallelism has not been without its critics. The French writer and philosopher Voltaire wondered whether two synchronised orchestras could manage without a conductor! It also seems rather uneconomical to assume that there are two totally different entities (i.e. the mind and the body). Another problem is that Leibnitz assumed every physical or bodily process had a mental counterpart, an assumption which seems unlikely to be true.

In spite of these difficulties, psychophysical parallelism subsequently became the accepted doctrine of several prominent German psychologists of the nineteenth and twentieth centuries, including Gustav Fechner, Wilhelm Wundt, and the Gestaltists. At any rate, Leibnitz did something to reduce the immense gulf between mind and body that had been proposed by Descartes.

The views of the philosopher Baruch Spinoza (1632–1677) initially attracted little attention, but ultimately became very influential. He put forward what has been called *double aspect theory*, according to which mental and physical processes are aspects of the same fundamental underlying reality: "The order and connection of ideas is the same as the order and connection of things".

A similar theory was proposed by the English philosopher Gilbert Ryle (1900–1976). He suggested that the distinction between mind and matter is essentially a grammatical one: mind is generally referred to by verbs, adverbs, or adjectives; whereas matter is referred to by nouns or pronouns. In other words, as Aristotle had argued, the mind simply consists of certain active physical processes within the body.

There are very definite advantages to double aspect theory. The problem of accounting for the inter-relationships between the mind and the body largely disappears if it is claimed that they are not separate entities. However, as Elizabeth Valentine (1982) pointed out, the theory suffers from a certain amount of vagueness. The precise nature of the "fundamental underlying reality" is not spelled out in any detail.

## The eighteenth century

You may remember that Aristotle argued that we can understand many of our thought processes in terms of the association of ideas. This viewpoint (often referred to as *associationism*) became very influential during the eighteenth century. Indeed, according to Murphy and Kovach (1972), "by the middle of the eighteenth century asssociationism had ... begun to be the central point around which psychological problems revolved" (p. 34). The seeds of the growing influence of associationism lay in the writings of the seventeenth-century philosophers Thomas Hobbes and John Locke, with the fruition coming in the work of David Hume (1739–1740) and David Hartley (1749).

According to Hume, the stream of thought consists of a multitude of experiences which combine and re-combine on associationistic principles. David Hartley developed this theory, and endeavoured to suggest a possible physiological basis of the association of ideas: each stimulus presented causes various nerve fibres in the brain to vibrate. If two stimuli occur in rapid succession, the vibrations caused by the first stimulus are followed by the vibrations caused by the second. These vibrations produce memory images of the stimuli. A subsequent presentation of the first stimulus will cause vibrations appropriate to it, followed by activation and vibration of the memory image associated with the second stimulus. This physiological ability for memory images to vibrate in the same order as the relevant past experiences provides a possible way to account for the association of ideas.

Reid (1785) and many other philosophers pointed out that there were profound limitations with associationism. It seems improbable that all thinking consists of an endless chain of associations produced by an essentially passive organism. Human thinking and reasoning extend well beyond simply being able to produce the most frequent or most recent associate of the stimulus we are currently experiencing. For example, we often use active strategies of thinking, which seem radically different to the mere association of ideas.

It is worth noting that the philosophers of the eighteenth century adopted an extremely narrow perspective on psychology. They were only interested in a few aspects of thinking, ignoring most of cognitive psychology, as well as social, developmental, comparative, and other perspectives on psychology. In addition, they attempted to clarify the processes involved in thinking without any recourse to experimental evidence.

# Understanding psychology

## Historical roots and current perspectives

Psychology, as it has evolved over the past 150 years or so, is related to several other disciplines, such as physiology, neurology, biology, sociology, biochemistry, medicine, and anthropology. The notion of regarding psychology as the meeting point of these different disciplines helps to explain both the complexity and the richness of contemporary psychology. This approach is adopted in Chapter 2, in which the historical roots of current perspectives (such as the biological, cognitive, social, and developmental) are also examined. It's not a case of some of these approaches being "right" and others "wrong"; rather, each approach succeeds in capturing part of the complex reality of human behaviour.

## Major issues

Psychology has probably been plagued by more philosophical and theoretical controversies than most other sciences. Some psychologists, for example, have argued that environmental influences are all-important in determining behaviour; whereas others have strongly emphasised the role of heredity. These disagreements constitute what is sometimes known as the *nature–nurture controversy*.

Another difference of opinion concerns whether or not we possess free will; some psychologists claim that the scientific approach to human behaviour must be based on the assumption that there is no such thing as free will. In Chapter 3 we look at these and other controversial topics.

## Motivation and emotion

Motivation and emotion are two of the most important and complex concepts in psychology. They are important because our behaviour is generally affected by our current emotional and motivational states. They are complex because our emotions and motives are determined by the physiological, cognitive, and behavioural systems in interaction with each other. These two key concepts are the focus of Chapter 4.

## Science and methods of research

It is generally agreed that amongst the major goals of science are "control" and "prediction". Most psychologists agree that psychology should be a scientific discipline, but some argue that a scientific approach is unsuited to the needs of psychology.

Various methods are open to psychologists carrying out research, although most psychological studies make use of the experimental method under laboratory conditions. This assumes that studying behaviour under controlled conditions is the best way of discovering which factors influence behaviour. However, it is also possible to carry out field experiments, applying experimental methods to a real-life situation.

The correlational method and single-case studies represent alternative approaches that can be used by researchers. Psychologists involved in clinical work argue that single-case studies based on a detailed investigation of individuals are more valuable than traditional studies involving comparisons between groups. In Chapter 5 we look at the advantages and disadvantages of different approaches to research, and examine the issues posed by different forms of data collection.

## Ethical issues

Many important issues need to be addressed by psychologists involved in carrying out research. Can the use of animals in psychological research be justified, for example? What forms of research can and cannot be justified at an ethical level? How do we ensure that all research is morally acceptable?

As with many other issues in psychology, there are no simple answers to these thorny questions. However, some of the relevant considerations in looking for answers are examined in Chapter 6.

# Summary

- There are various views about the nature of psychology. However, the majority opinion is that psychology is a *multi-disciplinary* subject with a predominantly *scientific* orientation.
- Its multi-disciplinary nature and the complexity of its subject matter (i.e. human beings) conspire to make psychology more difficult than most other scientific disciplines.
- Some critics argue that psychology is no more successful than common sense in providing an understanding of human behaviour. This argument is fatally flawed.
- There is no coherent commonsensical view of human behaviour, and most people are only modestly successful when they attempt to use common sense to predict the findings of psychological research.
- Psychology had its origins in Ancient Greece in the work of philosophers such as Socrates, Plato, and Aristotle.
- Descartes (1596–1650) argued that the mind or soul has no biological reality, and cannot be studied by the methods of science.
- Spinoza (1632–1677) proposed double aspect theory, according to which mental and physical processes are aspects of the same underlying reality.
- Associationism was very popular in the eighteenth century, but it is improbable that thinking usually consists of an endless chain of assocations produced by a passive organism.
- To understand psychology, it is helpful to study its historical roots and current perspectives, major issues, motivation and emotion, methods of research, and the ethical considerations involved.

## Further reading

For further study, a very readable account of the nature of contemporary psychology can be found in A.M. Colman's book *What is psychology? The inside story* (London, Hutchinson, 1988).

# Current approaches and historical roots

# 2

W e saw in Chapter 1 that philosophers have made several important contributions to psychology. One of the main themes of this chapter is that psychology has also been enriched by physiologists, neurologists, sociologists, zoologists, anthropologists, biologists, and others. It may seem strange that so many disciplines are of relevance to psychology. But there is some method in this madness.

Behaviour is determined by a wide variety of factors, so it can only be understood fully by taking account of contributions from scientists in other disciplines. As Beloff expressed it, "As soon as one attempts to say what psychology is about, it becomes clear one is dealing not with a single unified science, but with a collection of more or less loosely affiliated

THE SEARCH FOR A UNIFIED APPROACH TO PSYCHOLOGY CONTINUES...

disciplines each with its own peculiar concepts and laws, its own methods and techniques".

Although the most popular view regards psychology as an important multi-disciplinary science in its own right, some theorists have argued that it cannot be seen as a coherent science. According to Koch (1969, p. 64), psychology is such a fragmented subject because of the way in which it came into existence:

> Prior to the late nineteenth century, there are no precedents in the history of ideas for creating new fields of knowledge by edict. Sciences won their way to independence by achieving enough knowledge to become sciences. By the late nineteenth century, these justly discriminated fields of science had given such food to man's cognitive and material hungers as to make his appetite insatiable. At the same time, inquiry into the nature and trend of science itself began to focus into an apparently wholesome Victorian vision: that of a totally or-dered universe, totally open to the methods of science, and a totally ordered science, totally open to the stratagems—and wants—of man. It was against this background that psychol-ogy was stipulated into life.
>
> At the time of its inception, psychology was unique in the extent to which ... its methods preceded its problem ... The stipulation that psychology be adequate to science out-weighed the commitment that it be adequate to man.

Koch may be right that psychology as a coherent discipline did not exist at the end of the nineteenth century; but this was mainly because of its complex subject matter rather than its unrealistic adherence to the scien-tific method. Later on, the existence of various competing schools of psychology also added to the lack of coherence: the behaviourists, psy-choanalysts, and humanistic psychologists had very different ideas of the proper goals of psychology, and adopted very different methods to inves-tigate human behaviour and thinking.

In contemporary psychology, approaches to psychology are most clearly distinguished in terms of their subject matter, although there are also differences in the methods regarded as appropriate for investigating behaviour. The central concern of psychology is to understand behaviour, which is jointly determined by numerous very different factors:

- the specific stimuli presented to us
- our genetic endowment

- our physiological system
- our cognitive system
- the social environment
- the cultural environment
- our previous life experiences (including those of childhood)
- our personal characteristics (including intelligence, personality, and mental health).

It is impossible to provide an adequate explanation of behaviour if any of these factors is ignored, although, as we will see in this chapter, different approaches to psychology have emphasised one or other of them. Each approach will be considered in the context of its historical roots, in order to make clear its distinctive contribution to psychology.

# The psychoanalytic approach

## Historical roots

For many centuries, the treatment applied to those suffering from mental disease was positively barbaric. It was believed mental disorders were caused by demons or other supernatural forces. Popular "cures" for mental illness were based on the idea of making things as unpleasant as possible for the demon, to encourage him to escape, and included immersing the patient in boiling hot water, flogging, starvation, and torture.

Real progress in solving the mystery of the origins of mental illness was achieved by the Austrian mystic and physician Franz Mesmer (1734–1815). He treated patients suffering from various complaints by sitting them around a tub containing magnetised iron filings with protruding iron rods. It was claimed that cures were produced by the "animal magnetism" generated by this bizarre arrangement. Subsequently, however, it became clear that the sleeplike or hypnotic state involved in the exercise, rather than animal magnetism, was responsible for any cures.

One of the characteristics of the hypnotised state is a high level of suggestibility, and members of the French *Nancy School* such as Liebault and Bernheim claimed this was crucial in Mesmer's technique. They used the power of suggestion to cure mental illness, especially hysteria.

Members of the Nancy School also argued that suggestion could cause mental illness in the first place. For example, a patient who had been trapped in a derailed train developed hysterical paralysis of the legs, even though there was nothing physically wrong with them. The only plausible reasons for this hysterical paralysis was that it stemmed from the power of suggestion.

This work on animal magnetism and hypnosis had tremendous historical importance, for two reasons. First, it demonstrated that at least some
forms of mental illness could be treated successfully by psychological
rather than medical means. Second, it suggested that the unconscious
mind could have a powerful influence on the development of, and subsequent recovery from, mental illness. This idea was considerably
developed and extended by Sigmund Freud.

## Psychoanalysis

Sigmund Freud: 1856–1939. Photograph reproduced by permission of Mary Evans / Sigmund Freud Copyrights.

Sigmund Freud has had an
enormous impact on psy-
chology—even nowadays his
work is referred to in the psychological literature more
often than that of any other
psychologist. His fame rests
largely on his position as the
originator of *psychoanalysis*.
It is important to note that
psychoanalysis refers (1) to a
complex set of theories about
human emotional develop-
ment and (2) to a form of
treatment based in part on
those theoretical ideas.

Some of the richness of Freud's approach can be seen in his well-known
theory that the mind is divided into three parts: the *id*, which is the
repository of the sexual instinct; the *ego*, which is the conscious, rational
mind; and the *superego*, or conscience.

In a sense, this part of Freud's thinking represents a combination of a
theory of motivation, a cognitive theory, and a social psychological theory.
The id contains basic motivational forces; the ego corresponds to the
cognitive system; and the superego, or conscience, internalises the values
of family and of society generally.

Freud's theoretical work was immensely broad in coverage—amongst
other things, he proposed the first detailed theory of child development.

In essence, Freud suggested children normally go through a series of
developmental stages: first, the oral stage (pleasure is derived from activities involving the mouth); next comes the anal stage (based on the
processes involved in excretion); next comes the phallic stage, in which
pleasure is obtained from stimulation of the genitals; and development
culminates in the genital stage, in which pleasure is obtained by providing

bodily satisfaction to another person as well as to onself. If the child experiences problems at any of these stages (*fixates* is the technical term), it can have adverse effects later in life. If an adult becomes emotionally disturbed, he or she tends to return (or *regress*) to the stage of development at which fixation occurred during childhood. Freud thus put forward both a theory of child development, and an account of clinical disorders in which childhood experiences play an important part.

Freud is especially well-known for his theoretical views on mental disorders, which he thought were caused by conflicts between the id, ego, and superego. These conflicts could lead either to *neurosis* (such as anxiety disorders or neurotic depression); or to *psychosis* (such as schizophrenia or manic-depressive psychosis), in which there is some loss of contact with reality. In terms of Freudian theory, psychosis involves regression to an earlier stage of development than neurosis.

Why do neurotic individuals exhibit bizarre behaviour (agoraphobics, for example, are extremely reluctant to go into open spaces)? According to Freud, their odd behaviour prevents their level of anxiety from becoming threateningly high. Everyone (but especially neurotic individuals) forces threatening ideas into the unconscious by means of a process known as *repression*, or motivated forgetting. An important step in therapy is to make patients aware of important repressed information.

Psychoanalysis as a form of therapy is based on the assumption that the way to cure neurosis is to allow patients to gain access to their repressed ideas and conflicts from the fixated stage, and encourage them to face up to whatever emerges from the unconscious. Freud used the term *insight* to refer to these processes, and so the ultimate goal of psychoanalytic therapy is to provide the patient with insight. However, this is difficult to achieve because the emergence of extremely painful ideas and memories into consciousness produces a very high level of anxiety.

Freud used three main methods for recovering repressed ideas: hypnosis; free association; and dream analysis. He made less use of hypnosis as time went by, partly because it was difficult to hypnotise some patients. However, asking patients to think of associations to stimulus words (e.g. "father") as rapidly as possible appeared useful in tracking down repressed material, as did the careful interpretation of patients' dreams.

## Evaluation

Psychoanalysis has many successes to its credit. Although others had previously suggested that mental illness could be treated by psychological means, Freud was the first to develop a systematic form of psychological treatment for neurosis. This subsequently led on to several other forms of psychotherapy (e.g. neo-Freudian therapy; client-centred therapy).

Psychoanalysis was probably the first reasonably effective way of treating neurosis to be developed. H.J. Eysenck (1952) claimed that only 44% of patients receiving psychoanalysis recovered, compared with 66% of patients not receiving any treatment—implying that psychoanalysis actually reduces your chances of recovering! Subsequently, it became clear that psychoanalysis is generally considerably superior to having no treatment. For example, Bergin (1971) argued that the success rate for psychoanalysis was as high as 83%, which compares very favourably with a spontaneous recovery rate of only 30%.

Psychoanalytic theory also has some impressive successes to its credit. For example, the notion that childhood experiences play a part in determining adult behaviour is commonplace now, but was revolutionary when Freud first suggested it. Another example is the view that much important activity within the mind occurs below the conscious level, in the unconscious. There is now very strong evidence that a considerable amount of information processing is pre-conscious (see Chapter 3).

On the negative side, the unscientific approach adopted by Freud makes it difficult to test his theoretical views—and when his specific theories *have* been investigated, the evidence has been largely negative. Freud claimed, for example, that psychosis is simply more severe than neurosis; but it seems far more likely that psychosis and neurosis are actually very different forms of disorder. Another example is Freud's emphasis on repression: in spite of numerous attempts to demonstrate repression under laboratory conditions, there is still no convincing evidence of its existence.

So far as psychoanalytic therapy is concerned, there is the problem that we do not know in detail *why* it is effective. Freud argued that the information obtained from patients in the course of therapy demonstrated that psychoanalysis works because it is based on his theoretical ideas. However, this evidence is suspect, because there are grave dangers of contamination in the data obtained from patients: what the patient says may be influenced by what the therapist has said to him or her previously; and the therapist may use his or her theoretical preconceptions to interpret what the patient says in ways that distort it.

# The behaviourist approach

## Historical roots

The work of the biologist Jacques Loeb towards the end of the nineteenth century provided some of the impetus for the development of behaviourism. He studied plants, and focused on what are known as *tropisms*, or turning processes (some plants turn towards the light, whereas others turn away from it). This is a simple stimulus–response connection (e.g. light produces turning) which resembles the *stimulus–response associations* subsequently studied by the behaviourists. In addition, we can explain the plant's "behaviour" without needing to talk about complex internal processes, such as seeing. Work on tropisms by Loeb and other biologists confirmed the behaviourists in their view that it was unnecessary to speculate about internal psychological processes.

Behaviourism was also influenced by the *functionalist* school of psychology, initiated by the American philosopher and psychologist John Dewey (1859–1952) in 1896. The functionalists were impressed by Darwin's views on evolution, and the idea of "survival of the fittest". These views seemed to justify studying animal behaviour as a route to understanding human psychology, and led one of the functionalists (Edward Thorndike in 1898) to carry out one of the first ever animal experiments by a psychologist, studying the strategies adopted by cats trying to escape from a puzzle box.

Functionalists were interested in studying mental phenomena and behaviour in terms of their functional value in adapting the person or animal to its environment. They argued, for example, that the functional significance of consciousness is to make it easier for appropriate behaviour to be produced when simple, automatic behaviour patterns would be inadequate.

John B. Watson: 1878–1958. Photograph reproduced by permission of the Archives of the History of Psychology.

## Behaviourism

According to Watson (1913), "Psychology as the behaviourist views it is a purely objective, experimental branch of natural science. Its theoretical goal is the prediction and control of behaviour. Introspection forms no essential part of its method". It is interesting that Watson believed a major goal of psychology was to control behaviour—it helps explain the emphasis that behaviourists placed on investigating learning rather than other aspects of psychological functioning. If you want to change someone's behaviour, it is necessary to provide the appropriate learning experience.

It is important to note that behaviourism consisted of several different assumptions and beliefs. Initially, behaviourists tended to put forward negative assumptions, attacking much that was prevalent in psychology at the time. However, they subsequently developed a system of positive assumptions, amongst which the following are key:

- Subjectivity should be eliminated from psychology and replaced by a more objective approach, which involved abandoning introspection as a technique.
- Psychology should be the study of behaviour, because behaviour is objective and observable.
- The appropriate unit of analysis is the simple stimulus–response association, with complex behaviour involving numerous stimulus–response links.
- Behaviour is almost entirely determined by environmental factors rather than by heredity, making the study of learning fundamentally important to psychology. As Watson (1924) put it, "There is no such thing as an inheritance of capacity, talent, temperament, mental constitution and characteristics. These things depend on training that goes on mainly in the cradle".
- Learning can be understood in terms of conditioning principles.
- Compared with most previous theorists, there was less emphasis on the importance of the brain: "Though the brain remains a connecting station, it is for the behaviourist no more intelligible to say that we think with the brain than to say that we walk with the spinal cord" (Murphy & Kovach, 1972).

As can be seen from these assumptions, behaviourism was in part concerned with the methods that should be used in psychology (i.e. an emphasis on behaviour rather than on introspection); and in part involved the formulation of a theory of behaviour (the emphasis on conditioning, simple stimulus–response associations, and environmental determinants of behaviour). The theories of behaviour proposed by behaviourists (such as those of Pavlov, Tolman, and Skinner) were all somewhat narrow, being essentially theories of learning rather than of other aspects of human functioning.

## Evaluation

How valuable was the behaviourist approach to psychology? Their assumptions about methods still have value and relevance: it is generally agreed that careful observation of behaviour is of fundamental importance to psychology, although nowadays there is more emphasis on using behavioural measures to infer internal processes. The experimental method as advocated by the behaviourists was taken over (and extended) by cognitive psychologists, and cognitive psychology is at the centre of contemporary psychology.

In more general terms, behaviourism proved to be of lasting importance because of its insistence that psychology should be a properly scientific discipline. Psychologists in Germany and elsewhere had previously carried out psychological experiments in a scientific fashion, but the behaviourists spelled out more systematically than anyone had before exactly how psychology could achieve scientific status.

The main danger with the behaviourists' insistence on careful observation of the effects of well-controlled manipulations of the stimulus situation on behaviour, was that of artificiality. For example, Watson and the other early behaviourists were very impressed by Pavlov's experiments on dogs, which learned to salivate to the sound of a tone that had previously been associated with the presentation of food. Although this demonstration of conditioning is of importance, the dogs participating in these experiments were generally put in a restraining harness in the laboratory. It seems improbable that much could be learned about dogs' normal behaviour in such artificial and restricted conditions.

The theory of behaviour proposed by the behaviourists is now of marginal importance—due in part to the lack of validity of many of their assumptions (for example, that learning consists only of stimulus–response associations; that heredity is largely irrelevant; and that conditioning principles can account for all learning). In essence, the behaviourists assumed that behaviour is determined almost entirely by external stimuli, whereas in reality it is usually determined by internal factors (e.g. past knowledge and experience; motivation) as well as by the immediate situation.

A major problem with many behaviourist theories is that they were grossly over-simplified. For example, Watson argued that thinking was merely sub-vocal speech, which led the philosopher Herbert Feigl to remark wittily that Watson "made up his windpipe that he had no mind". Watson's position was disproved in a rather dangerous study carried out by Smith, Brown, Toman, and Goodman (1947). Smith was given a drug that paralysed his entire musculature, and he had to be kept alive by using an artificial respirator. This temporary paralysis prevented him from engaging in sub-vocal speech or any other bodily movement, and so should have rendered him incapable of thought. In fact, he reported that he had been able to observe what was going on around him, to comprehend other people's speech, and to think about these events while in the paralysed state.

Perhaps the main example of behaviourism as a theory continuing to have a major influence is *behaviour therapy* (discussed more fully later). This is an approach to the treatment of mental disorders based largely on conditioning principles.

The general rejection of the theories proposed by the behaviourists is also partly due to the limitations of the data they collected. They obtained most of their experimental data from species such as rats, dogs, and pigeons, but were perfectly content to claim that their findings had immediate relevance to human behaviour—which is dubious.

# The approach of abnormal psychology

## Historical roots

Some of the historical roots of abnormal psychology have already been discussed. Sigmund Freud, with the development of psychoanalysis, was the first person to provide a systematic form of therapy based squarely on psychological principles. Several other forms of *psychotherapy* (therapy based on changing cognitive processes and structures) were developed subsequently. These include the neo-Freudian approach of Adler, Fromm, and others, all of whom argued that neurosis is caused more by social factors than by the biological actors emphasised by Freud. Another form of psychotherapy is Rogers' *client-centred therapy* (discussed later in the chapter), which started to become popular during the 1950s and 1960s.

Another major historical influence on contemporary abnormal psychology came from behaviourism, and in the 1960s resulted in *behaviour therapy*. In essence, behaviour therapists argue that abnormal behaviour occurs as a result of learning, and that further learning can result in the elimination of that behaviour. More specifically, it is assumed that the principles of conditioning that were originally demonstrated in other species are relevant to the human species, and that the learning and unlearning of abnormal forms of behaviour occur through conditioning.

Two brief examples will be given here. First, there is *aversion therapy*, which involves reducing or eliminating undesirable behaviour by following it almost immediately with an extremely unpleasant stimulus. For instance, alcoholic patients are given a drug so that every time they take a sip of an alcoholic drink, they are violently sick. This is usually effective in reducing drinking behaviour, but the effects often disappear after the patients stop taking the drug.

Second, there is the *token economy,* which is based on the notion that behaviour that is followed by reward or reinforcement will be more likely to be repeated in future. Ayllon and Azrin (1968) studied female patients who had been hospitalised for an average of 16 years. They were given plastic tokens for carrying out chores such as making their beds or combing their hair; these tokens could then be exchanged for rewards such as seeing a film or paying an extra visit to the canteen. Use of this token economy increased the average number of chores carried out by each patient each day from five to more than forty.

A third historical influence stemmed from the view that abnormal behaviour is caused by underlying organic problems, which can best be treated by means of bodily manipulations. For example, severely depressed patients over the past 50 years or so have been given a form of treatment known as *electroconvulsive shock treatment* (ECT), involving a fairly strong electric current being passed between two electrodes, one on each side of the patient's forehead. ECT is often reasonably effective, but it can produce unwanted side-effects, such as memory loss.

## Current perspective

Most of the forms of therapy currently in use have developed out of the historical approaches discussed earlier. So far as psychotherapy is concerned, a major development over the past 20 years or so has been the increased use of *cognitive therapy*. Cognitive therapists such as Aaron Beck and Albert Ellis argue that anxious and depressed patients suffer from self-defeating cognitive beliefs and thoughts (such as "I must be successful all the time for people to respect me" or "I cannot cope with everyday life"). These irrational beliefs can be changed by challenging patients to justify them or by giving patients re-attribution training, in which they learn to accept that many of the problems in their lives stem from factors outside their control.

Cognitive therapy resembles psychoanalysis in that the emphasis is on changing the patient's ways of thinking. However, cognitive therapy focuses very largely on the patient's current concerns and beliefs, whereas psychoanalysis argues for the importance of past experiences. In addition, psychoanalysis attaches great significance to the unconscious mind, whereas cognitive therapy is based largely on what is immediately available to consciousness.

Cognitive therapy (unlike psychoanalysis) has links with behaviour therapy, in that it is accepted that behaviour must be changed if the patient is to recover fully. Some ingredients of cognitive therapy are primarily designed to alter behaviour. For example, depressed patients sometimes engage in *activity raising* (in which they are rewarded for increased involvement in activities) and *graded task assignment* (in which they are given specific tasks to perform in their everyday lives).

According to conditioning theory, most learning happens in a relatively automatic way and does not depend on the learner's cognitive processes. There is increasing evidence that cognitive processes are often very important, and behaviour therapists now accept that cognitive factors need to be taken into account.

For example, Lick (1975) reported a study on *systematic desensitisation*, a form of therapy in which patients with a phobia (extreme fear) of some object or situation (such as spiders) learn to respond in a relaxed fashion while progressively more frightening stimuli relating to their phobia are presented to them. Lick told his patients that he would present phobic stimuli subliminally (so fast they could not be seen consciously), and they were presented with physiological feedback allegedly indicating that they were becoming more successful in remaining relaxed when presented with these stimuli. In fact, no stimuli were presented and the physiological feedback was fake.

Because Lick's procedure differed markedly from the one advocated by behaviour therapists, they would expect this mock treatment to be ineffective. In fact it worked well, presumably because cognitive change was produced—the patients believed they could control their fear of phobic stimuli.

There has been an increase in forms of therapy based on bodily manipulations, and the term *somatic therapy* is sometimes used as a general term to describe them. Most forms of somatic therapy involve the use of drugs, and there have been progressive improvements in the drugs available. Take the case of clinical anxiety. Until 30 years ago, barbiturates were often prescribed for anxious patients. Barbiturates certainly reduce anxiety, but they can cause addiction and marked loss of concentration. During the 1960s, they were replaced by benzodiazepines such as Valium and Librium, in part because they have fewer side-effects. However, the benzodiazepines can cause sleepiness and some memory loss. In the last few years, new anti-anxiety drugs such as buspirone have been developed. These drugs offer the prospect of fewer unwanted side-effects than either the benzodiazepines or the barbiturates.

Patients taking drugs can often lead fairly normal lives, but a major limitation is that most drugs do not directly help to produce a cure. Another problem is that patients often suffer *withdrawal symptoms* when a course of drug treatment comes to an end. For example, an anxious patient whose level of anxiety has been low while taking anti-anxiety drugs may find it very difficult to cope subsequently when his or her anxiety level goes up sharply. Because of this, many experts believe that anti-anxiety drugs should only be prescribed for short periods to allow patients to get through a short-lived personal crisis.

## Evaluation

On the face of it, a simple way of establishing that abnormal psychology has made significant progress would be to demonstrate that ever higher percentages of patients are now recovering. However, it is notoriously difficult to define "recovery" in a precise fashion, and account obviously needs to be taken of the initial severity of the patient's condition. On top of that, it might be misleading to assume that patients who recover after, for example, behaviour therapy have recovered because of the application of conditioning principles. As Davison and Neale (1986, p. 475) pointed out, "All therapies derive at least some of their power from the faith that people have in the healer".

Although it is difficult to establish exactly how successful any given form of therapy is in producing recovery, there is rather strong evidence that all of the major forms of therapy are reasonably effective. For example, Elkin et al. (1986) compared the effectiveness of cognitive therapy, drug therapy, interpersonal therapy (focusing on interpersonal relationships), and placebo (an inactive drug). The recovery rate was over 50% with cognitive therapy, drug therapy, and interpersonal therapy, compared with a figure of 29% for the placebo patients who didn't receive any proper treatment.

Clinical psychologists have developed greater theoretical understanding of the various conditions and how to treat them. For example, it has been established that cognitive factors play an important role in the success of behaviour therapy. There has also been an increase in the range of therapies available. This means that if clinical psychologists discover that a particular form of therapy is not working well with a given patient, they have more alternative forms of treatment to fall back on.

On the negative side, it is important to note that abnormal psychology has not contributed much to our understanding of normal individuals. In principle, it might be thought that our developing understanding of abnormality and the extremes of behaviour found in clinical patients would be of use in normal psychology, but this hasn't really been the case. Instead, clinical psychology has benefited greatly from advances in other areas of psychology (such as behaviourism and cognitive psychology). In other words, the main direction of influence has been from our knowledge of normal human functioning to abnormal psychology rather than the other way around.

# The biological approach

## Historical roots

It is difficult for us to imagine the enormous impact that *Origin of species* by Charles Darwin (1809–1882) had on the way people think about themselves. Before its publication in 1859, people had generally assumed that only human beings have souls, and so we are radically different from other

Charles Darwin: 1809–1882. A 19th century cartoon showing Charles Darwin and a French physician, Littre, using the agility received from their primate ancestors to break through ignorance and credulity. Picture courtesy Jean-Loup Charmet/Science Photo Library.

species. The notion that human beings had evolved out of other species meant this inflated view of the importance of the human species had to be re-assessed. Many people found it extremely difficult to come to terms with the idea that human beings should be regarded simply as members of the animal kingdom.

Even though Darwin was a biologist and not a psychologist, his views on evolution had several major implications for psychology. First, and most important, psychologists began to realise that it was worth considering human psychology from the biological perspective. The most prominent psychologist to do so was Sigmund Freud, whose emphasis on the sex drive would have been almost unthinkable pre-Darwin.

Second, it was now clear that the study of animals could be of great relevance in attempting to understand human behaviour, and this led to the development of comparative or animal psychology.

Third, Darwin emphasised the importance of heredity, and the idea that offspring tend to resemble their parents. This suggested to psychologists that the role of heredity in influencing human behaviour should be explored.

Fourth, Darwin focused on variation among the members of a species, with evolution selectively favouring some members rather than others (the survival of the fittest). This led to a re-awakening of interest in individual differences, and ultimately to the study of personality and intelligence.

## Current perspective: Human sociobiology

Edward Wilson (1975) argued that the biological approach favoured by Darwin could be extended to provide an understanding of social behaviour; this produced what is generally known as *human sociobiology*. The key assumption of human sociobiologists is that "individuals should act to maximise their inclusive fitness. Inclusive fitness refers to the number of descendants left in future generations, including those of relatives as well as direct descendants" (Smith, 1983, p. 224). The goal of gene survival is allegedly involved when humans weigh up the benefits and costs of different forms of social behaviour. A mother who is willing to die to ensure the survival of her children (and who is thus demonstrating altruism or unselfishness) can be said to be acting so as to maximise the chances of the survival of her family's genes.

Human sociobiology has some successes to its credit, and we will consider two examples here. In many societies, the mother's brother plays a much more active role in bringing up her child than does the father. If there is reasonable chance that the husband is not the father, then the genetic link between the mother's brother and the child will often be greater than that between the "father" and the child. It follows from the sociobiological perspective that the mother's brother should have more of an investment in the child.

The second example concerns the strange finding that the average weight of newborn babies is somewhat less than it should be to maximise the chances of their survival. This is difficult to explain, but sociobiologists have argued that it helps to preserve the mother's resources, to enhance her chances of having further children.

Human sociobiology has certainly proved provocative. Many feel that it is in danger of slipping over into racism with its emphasis on maximising the number of descendants of one's own group, possibly at the expense of other groups. Although these dangers are real and must be recognised, it is still possible to evaluate human sociobiology in the same way as any other theory.

At the purely scientific level, there are grave doubts as to the general adequacy of human sociobiology. Most psychologists believe that human social behaviour is influenced much more by the development of knowledge and culture than it is by pure heredity or biological factors. There are also several aspects of Western society that seem inconsistent with socio-biology. For example, the average family size in many countries has gone down in spite of increasing prosperity, which is contrary to the notion of maximising the survival of one's genes. Another example is the fact that most adoptions take place outside the family. This substantial investment of resources is inexplicable in terms of the survival of one's family genes.

Smith (1983) reached a reasonable conclusion in his critical review of human sociobiology: "It seems likely that 'naive' human sociobiology has most relevance to earlier phases of human evolution, and to less complex societies, and has a much more limited application in its unmodified form to modern industrial societies" (p. 240).

## Evaluation

The fact that human sociobiology has proved of little value in under-standing human behaviour does not invalidate the biological approach to psychology. Comparative psychology and physiological psychology (dis-cussed in the next two sections) both fall within the general area of the biological approach, and have proved to be of great value. In addition, although more controversially, the study of genetic factors in intelligence and personality (discussed later in the chapter) have contributed to our understanding of individual differences.

# Comparative psychology

## Historical roots

The dominant approach to the study of animal or comparative psychology until the 1950s was that of the behaviourists, who typically studied ani-mals under rather artificial laboratory conditions, and were relatively unconcerned about possible differences among species.

A number of European scientists, in particular Niko Tinbergen and Konrad Lorenz, proposed a very different approach to the study of animals, known as *ethology*. The ethological approach involves studying animals in their natural habitat rather than in the laboratory: under natural conditions, the enormous diversity of behaviour from one species to another becomes apparent. The ethological approach also differed from previous animal research in its use of *observational methods*: detailed observations were made of the animals' behaviour, and there was less emphasis on the manipulation of the environment characterising the experimental method.

Part of the impetus for the ethological approach came from Darwin's theory of evolution. According to Darwin's theory, survival of an individual or a species depends on its adaptation or adjustment to the environment. As a consequence, as the ethologists realised, our understanding of both individuals and entire species is enriched by considering their natural environment.

The ethologists also placed a Darwinian emphasis on *instincts* (innate capacities or patterns of responding), the most famous example of which is *imprinting*. There is a genetically determined tendency for newborn members of certain species (such as geese and ducks) to follow the first moving object they encounter, and to continue to follow that object every time it appears. Of course, the first moving object seen by most newborn ducks and geese is their mother, so imprinting makes a lot of evolutionary sense. However, Lorenz found that newborn greylag geese would follow him if he ensured that he was the first moving object they saw.

Konrad Lorenz with a greylag goose.
Photo courtesy *Radio Times.*

According to Lorenz (1935), imprinting occurs only during a short critical period early in life; it is irreversible, and is found only in certain ground-nesting birds. In fact, as Gross (1992) has pointed out, none of these assumptions is correct. Imprinting can occur at times other than shortly after birth, although that period is one of particular sensitivity. The effects of imprinting can sometimes be reversed or undone; and imprinting-like phenomena are observable in a wide range of species.

Ethology began to have an impact within European psychology during the 1930s and 1940s, but took longer to have any real influence in the United States. The initial lack of American interest was due partially to the theoretical chasm between behaviourism and ethology; and partially to the fact that behaviourists favoured very rigorous and precise experimentation, whereas ethologists tended to carry out relatively uncontrolled studies. Ultimately, however, the insights of the ethologists combined fruitfully with the experimental rigour of the behaviourists.

Ethology has also influenced the development of human psychology: more and more psychologists believe human behaviour should be studied under natural conditions, rather than artificially in a laboratory (see Chapter 5). This is, of course, precisely what ethologists argued with regard to animal behaviour. Heather (1976) addressed the problems of traditional approaches to studying human behaviour, and concluded: "What we need … is an ethology of human life" (p. 32).

Probably the best-known example of ethology influencing human psychology is Lorenz's (1966) work on aggression in the form of attacks on other members of the same species. In essence, he argued that aggression in other species is well-regulated and can actually be constructive, whereas human aggression can be extremely destructive.

Aggression in other species is controlled by means such as *ritualisation* and *appeasement rituals*. Ritualisation refers to aggression expressed in a stereotyped fashion, so death and/or injury are rare. For example, when two wolves fight, the loser exposes its jugular vein, which brings the fight to an end. Appeasement rituals are designed to prevent a fight starting in the first place. Lorenz accepted that humans manifest signs of ritualisation and appeasement rituals, and cited smiling and begging for forgiveness as human appeasement rituals. However, our development of technology (such as rifles and bombs) means that the killer and the victim, or victims, are often very far apart. As a consequence, the rituals that are so effective in other species cannot be used. In addition, Lorenz believed that biological factors have made humans extremely aggressive.

Although Lorenz's theory of aggression has been very influential, it is clearly over-simplified. The human species is by no means the only one in which members kill others of the same species: male lions taking over a group or pride of lions, for example, frequently kill all the cubs in the pride. Another weakness of Lorenz's theory is his assumption that aggression is almost entirely determined by biological factors. In fact, as the work of anthropologists such as Margaret Mead and others has indicated, the amount of aggression and the ways in which it is manifested vary considerably from one culture to another. This suggests learning and cultural experience are far more important than was admitted by Lorenz.

## Current perspective

A crucial issue within comparative psychology concerns the extent to which the findings obtained from other species can be generalised to humans. It is clear that there are some important differences among species, especially in terms of how much of their behaviour is *pre-programmed* (determined by heredity). Lower species (such as ants and bees) are much more pre-programmed than higher species (such as humans and apes). For example, honey bees naturally perform a rather complicated "wagging" dance, which provides information to other bees about the direction and distance away of a food supply. In contrast, humans have to learn most of the skills they possess in a laborious fashion; however, the lack of pre-programming means we can respond flexibly to new or changing environments.

There are both major similarities and differences between humans and other species, some of which can be understood in the context of a theory proposed by P.D. McLean (1973). He argued that the human brain consists of three parts:

- the *reptile brain*—the brain stem and lower part of the brain, concerned with basic functions such as breathing;
- the *paleocortex* or *limbic system*—the part of the brain concerned with the emotions;
- the *neocortex*—the top part of the brain, concerned with language and reasoning.

In general terms, similarities between humans and other species are most marked for those aspects of behaviour based on the reptile brain or the paleocortex. In contrast, no other species has developed a neocortex resembling that found in humans, and thus large differences between us and other species tend to be found for behaviour determined by the neocortex.

Evidence consistent with the view that the paleocortex or limbic system functions similarly in many different species was reviewed by Gray (1985). He focused on the emotion of anxiety in several species ranging from goldfish to humans. Anti-anxiety drugs (e.g. benzodiazepines such as Librium and Valium) have similar effects in every species, reducing fearful responses to threatening situations. This led Gray (1985) to conclude: "Anxiety in man and anxiety in animals must have the same basic neurology, because the two respond to the same drugs" (p. 103).

Further research was carried out, in which cuts or lesions were made in parts of the limbic system of various species (but not humans for obvious ethical reasons). This research revealed that cuts to the *septo-hippocampal system* produce effects on behaviour closely resembling the effects of anti-anxiety drugs. This suggests that the septo-hippocampal system plays a major role in anxiety in several different species including humans, which is an important contribution to our understanding of human anxiety.

The notion that other species are very different from ours when it comes to higher mental processes (such as language) may seem inconsistent with the well-known work of Allen and Beatrice Gardner. In 1966, they began to train a young female chimpanzee called Washoe to use a modified version of American Sign Language, a gesture-based language used by deaf people. After three-and-a-half years, Washoe had apparently mastered the rudiments of language. She could sign a total of 132 words, and could combine signs in a meaningful way: when asked, "What that?", in the presence of a swan, she replied, "water bird".

Washoe's performance was hailed at the time as showing that language is not unique to humans. However, it is generally agreed now that chimpanzees are incapable of proper language learning. For example, a chimpanzee called Nim Chimpsky learned 125 signs for words in four years. However, the average length of his communications never exceeded about 1.5 signs (Terrace, 1979), which compares unfavourably against that of very young children. Even his longer communications contained relatively little meaning, as can be seen in his longest-ever communication: "Give orange me give eat orange me eat orange give me eat orange give me you".

## Evaluation

As we have seen, the comparative approach is particularly valuable when it comes to studying lower processes, but less useful in terms of shedding light on high cognitive abilities. In addition, there are various practical advantages associated with the use of other species in research. Experiments that could not possibly be carried out on humans for ethical reasons (e.g. those involving surgical procedures) can sometimes be performed on animals. However, there have (quite appropriately) been increasingly great restrictions on animal experimentation recently (see Chapter 6).

There are also practical advantages if one wants to study the processes of development or to observe inter-generational similarities and dissimilarities. Most other species have a much shorter period of development than humans, and also reproduce at much younger ages. It would often exceed the life span of the experimenter to conduct a study of changes from one generation to the next in humans.

# The psychophysiological approach

## Historical roots

Johannes Muller (1801–1858) and Hermann von Helmholtz (1821–1894) both made enormous contributions to physiological psychology in Germany. Among Muller's major contributions was the publication of a three-volume textbook of physiology between the years 1833 and 1840. In this textbook he argued that the perceptions we have in our various senses (such as vision, hearing, etc.) are radically different from each other, and this may well occur because some nerves are specialised to give us vision, others are specialised to provide hearing, and so on. Muller speculated that different parts of the brain might also be specialised to provide us with visual perception, auditory perception, and so on; but decided on balance (and incorrectly) against that view.

The great importance of Muller's theoretical views was the suggestion that there were very strong links between the mind and the body. More specifically, in order to understand why we perceive the world in the way we do, it is essential to take account of the physiology of the nervous system.

Hermann von Helmholtz was a physicist, mathematician, and psychologist as well as a physiologist. He was interested in perception, at least in part because "the physiology of the senses is a border land in which the two great divisions of human knowledge, natural and mental science, encroach on one another's domain; in which problems arise which are important to both, and which only the combined labour of both can solve."

Helmholtz is best known for his work on vision and on hearing. He proposed a theory according to which there are three fundamental colours (red, green, and blue). It was assumed that each of these fundamental colours had its own physiological basis in the form of receptor mechanisms in the eye. This view was backed up by experimental evidence, but cannot be regarded as a complete account.

After this promising start, and the important work by Pavlov on salivation in dogs, physiological psychology went through a somewhat barren period. As Thomson (1968) concluded his discussion of physiological psychology between the two World Wars: "In spite of much admirable work in physiology during this period, there was not much which could directly throw light on behaviour. At the same time, psychologists were inclined to be less concerned with physiology than in earlier, and later, periods" (p. 285).

An important exception was the work of Walter Cannon (1871–1945). His book, *Bodily changes in pain, hunger, fear and rage*, was published in 1929, and has had a major impact on the study of emotion (see Chapter 4). He argued that the sympathetic branch of the autonomic nervous system is active in fear and rage, whereas the parasympathetic branch is active in emotions such as joy and tranquillity. He also emphasised the role played by hormones such as adrenaline in fear and rage. In general terms, he greatly clarified the role of the physiological system in states of emotion.

## Current perspective

The relationship between physiology and psychology has changed over the years. Originally, most research involved observing the effects of some physiological manipulation (such as a cut or lesion in the brain) on behaviour. Research of this kind is now largely confined to non-human species, and may be referred to as *physiological psychology*.

In contrast, most research nowadays involves studing the inter-relationships between the physiological and psychological aspects of behaviour. For example, we can try to increase our understanding of dreaming by taking various physiological measures of people while they are asleep (see Chapter 3). The term *psychophysiology* is often used to describe such research, in which physiological measures are used as dependent variables.

Contemporary psychophysiology has been influenced by a number of related disciplines. For example, physiology and biochemistry have become increasingly important sciences, and both have contributed techniques and ideas that have been of value in the development of psychophysiology.

That part of psychophysiology which is potentially of greatest importance is concerned with the cognitive functioning of the brain. Until comparatively recently, one of the few physiological techniques available for studying the brain was the *electroencephalogram* or EEG. This has been used, for example, to study the activity of the brain during sleep, where it has revealed the existence of five different stages of sleep characterised by different patterns of brain-wave activity (see Chapter 3 for a more detailed account).

The major problem with the standard EEG is that it provides a rather gross measure of brain activity, and so doesn't permit precise identification of the part or parts of the brain from which the activity comes. The reason is that the EEG is recorded from the scalp rather than from the brain itself, leading some psychologists to compare the technique to trying to follow a conversation in the next room by putting your ear to the wall!

Clearer information about brain functioning comes from the *evoked response potential* (ERP), in which a stimulus is presented several times, and EEG recordings are taken. These recordings are then averaged so that activity produced by the stimulus can be distinguished from spontaneous activity of the brain.

There is plentiful evidence from studies of selective attention that averaged ERPs to attended stimuli are greater than those to unattended stimuli. Of more interest is the finding that the enhanced response to attended stimuli occurs within 70 milliseconds of stimulus onset (Loveless, 1983), suggesting that the discrimination between attended and unattended stimuli is made very rapidly.

Another method of investigating brain activity is based on the measurement of *regional cerebral blood flow*, using a small amount of radioactive substance injected into the blood stream. A scanner relays information about levels of radioactivity to a computer, which displays the information in the form of a coloured map revealing radioactivity levels in the various areas of the brain. There is greater blood flow to more active areas of the brain, and thus higher levels of radioactivity.

This technique was used by Tulving (1989) to compare *episodic* or *autobiographical memory*, and *semantic memory* (our knowledge of facts and meanings, such as knowing that Paris is the capital of France). There has been some controversy as to whether episodic and semantic memory differ in terms of the processes involved, as well as in terms of their content. Tulving discovered there was relatively more activity towards the front of the brain when episodic rather than semantic memories were being retrieved, whereas there was more activity towards the back of the brain with semantic memories. Although these data are preliminary, they suggest that episodic and semantic memory may involve quite different processes and structures.

A related method is *positron emission tomography* (PET), which involves using a ring of gamma ray detectors (the PET scanner) to detect emitted positrons (anti-particles of electrons) in the brain following injection of oxygen-15 labelled water into the blood. This technique was used by Petersen et al. (1988) to study the processing of words. They discovered different highly localised areas of brain activity associated with visual and auditory word presentation, speech production, and the processing of meaning. The exciting implication is that there are close correspondences between mental operations and their biological bases in the brain, and that these correspondences can be revealed by PET scans.

## Evaluation

The psychophysiological approach has proved very valuable in the study of emotion and motivation. However, recent technological advances suggest that the most progress within the psychophysiological approach in the next few years may well come in the study of cognitive processes in the brain. Most of the current techniques are somewhat limited, because they only show the amounts of activity in different parts of the brain averaged over a 30–60 second period. However, techniques that are now being developed will allow us to observe brain activity on a continuous basis, which should increase our understanding of how the brain works.

There are substantial methodological problems with psychophysiology. Physiological measures are affected by many factors, including the time of day, the characteristics of the experimenter, the temperature of the experimental room, and so on, as well as by the independent variable identified by the experimenter. For example, Christie and Brearty (1981) found that physiological measures for male and female subjects were comparable when the experimenter was female, but male subjects showed less physiological reactivity than female subjects when the experimenter was male. All of these complexities mean that it can be difficult to interpret the findings obtained.

A second problem with psychophysiology is the fact that the situations used are typically very artificial. Subjects often have to sit as still as possible in a laboratory while wired up to bulky equipment—a situation that obviously differs considerably from most real-life situations. As a result of technological advances—some of them stemming from the American space programme—much smaller and lighter pieces of apparatus have been designed, so that physiological recordings can be made as the subjects walk around and pursue their normal activities. However, it is still too early to be sure whether all of the previous problems have been eliminated.

Third, there is the problem that most psychophysiological measures are rather indirect. For example, heart rate, respiration rate, and galvanic skin response (sweating) are all used to measure autonomic activity, but unfortunately they typically only correlate modestly with each other. Part of the reason for this is *response specificity* (Lacey, 1967)—most people respond more strongly on some measures than on others, but individuals differ in terms of their most and least responsive measures.

Fourth, although psychophysiology has much to contribute to areas such as motivation, emotion, and cognition, it is less clear if it is of much value in areas such as social psychology. For example, our understanding of the behaviour of crowds, or the ways in which social attitudes develop, would probably not have been increased to any great extent by making use of physiological measures.

# Individual differences

## Historical roots

The systematic investigation of individual differences started with the work of Sir Francis Galton (1822–1911), who was a cousin of Charles Darwin. The publication of Galton's book *Hereditary genius* in 1869 was a landmark in the study of individual differences, with the previous lack of interest in the subject being rather surprising. As Murphy and Kovach (1972) pointed out, "Individual differences had not been seriously treated before as part of the subject matter of psychology. Perhaps their neglect had been the most extraordinary blind spot in previous formal psychology. It was Darwinism, rather than the previous history of psychology, which brought about an interest in the problem" (p. 138).

Galton was the first psychologist to develop what may be regarded as an intelligence test. However, the test focused on simple tasks such as reaction time, and didn't provide a satisfactory assessment of intelligence.

A key aspect of Galton's approach (probably influenced by Darwin) was a belief in the importance of heredity. This led him to claim that there are specific forms of inherited genius; allegedly seen in the tendency for specific families to produce several eminent scientists, lawyers, authors, or whatever. However, it could plausibly be argued that environmental influences are also very important, because children born into a distinguished family are likely to have advantages and opportunities denied to many other children.

In 1876, Galton investigated the relative importance of heredity and environment in intelligence by studying a number of fraternal and identical twins—the first time that a proper twin study had been carried out. He was very struck by the degree of similarity that existed between identical twins: "The impression that all this evidence leaves on the mind is one of some wonder whether nurture can do anything at all, beyond giving instruction and professional training … There is no escape from the conclusion that nature prevails enormously over nurture when the differences of nurture do not exceed what is commonly to be found among persons of the same rank of society and in the same country". Such a statement would be regarded nowadays as either very contentious or downright wrong.

Francis Galton: 1822–1911. Photograph courtesy Archives of the History of American Psychology.

Intelligence testing was developed by the Frenchman Alfred Binet (1857–1911). In 1904, the French Ministry of Public Instruction appointed a committee to consider the education of mentally retarded children. This led Binet to devise an intelligence test to identify such children at an early age, so they could receive special educational treatment. This test focused on complex cognitive processes and provided a better method of assessing individual differences in intelligence than that previously used by Galton.

## Current perspective

Strictly speaking, research on individual differences includes comparisons between children of different ages, clinical case studies, and studies on particular brain-damaged patients. However, here we will consider only individual differences in intelligence and personality.

Psychometrics (the design and use of psychological tests) has continued to form an important part of the individual differences approach. It is essential to have a good theoretical understanding of the structure of intelligence and personality in order to devise good tests. Much of that theoretical understanding has come from the use of *factor analysis*.

In the case of intelligence, the general strategy is to give numerous tests to large groups of individuals, and then to inter-correlate the scores. It is assumed that tests which correlate highly with each other are measuring approximately the same intellectual ability; whereas those which don't correlate are measuring different abilities. Factor analysis is a statistical technique based on those assumptions, providing evidence about the underlying structure of intelligence. Precisely the same logic is applied to the statistical analysis of personality questionnaires.

There is now reasonable agreement that intelligence has a hierarchical structure. For example, Carroll (1986) re-analysed many of the findings from factor-analytic studies of intelligence tests, and concluded that there are three levels in the hierarchy: a general factor at the top; seven factors of intermediate generality (such as general speed and memory capacity) in the middle; and numerous highly specific factors at the bottom.

The position is very similar in the case of personality: theorists such as Guilford, Cattell, and H.J. Eysenck have all used the factor-analytic approach to uncover the factors contained in personality tests, but have disagreed on the structure of personality. More recent research has suggested there are five major factors of personality (sometimes known as the Big Five), named by McCrae and Costa (1985) as extraversion, agreeableness, conscientiousness, neuroticism, and openness.

### Evaluation

Research into individual differences has been very valuable in establishing the hierarchical structure of intelligence, and the major factors or traits of personality. Most of the tests that have been devised are reasonably high in both reliability (consistency) and validity (measuring what the test claims to measure). These are impressive achievements, and have had a substantial impact on our understanding of individual differences.

On the negative side, there are doubts as to whether the psychometricians are correct in assuming that intelligence and personality remain relatively unchanged over long periods of time. The doubts about personality are particularly great, because there is reasonably strong evidence that an individual's personality can change considerably over time.

Another doubt concerns the relevance to everyday life of intelligence as measured by standard tests. There are many streetwise or politically skilful individuals who succeed extremely well in life even though their tested intelligence is relatively modest. This suggests that the concept of intelligence should be broadened to include more of the skills that permit individuals to cope with the complexities of modern society.

# Social psychology

## Historical roots

Social psychology was one of the last areas of psychology to be fully accepted. As Thomson (1968) says in his historical review, "Social psychology did not become sufficiently coherent and technically advanced to receive much recognition until after the Second World War" (p. 370). Of course, there were some attempts to adopt a social psychological perspective many years earlier than that. For example, in the 1890s, Le Bon discussed crowd behaviour. He emphasised the notion that individuals in crowds can be highly suggestible and so behave in ways that are irrational and out of keeping with their normal behaviour.

Floyd Allport published his influential book *Social psychology* in 1924. Much of this book was given over to the issue of the ways in which an individual's behaviour differs when he or she is alone compared to in the presence of others. For example, he discovered that many simple tasks were completed faster when performed in a group situation, and he claimed that this was due to *social facilitation*. Allport focused on individual behaviour in social situations, rather than on distinctively social processes such as group dynamics in small groups, and it was only much later that such processes became a central focus of social psychology.

## Current perspective

Contemporary social psychology is based on the fact that we are social animals. We continually interact with other people, and our behaviour is much influenced by the presence of others—as illustrated by research on conformity and obedience to authority. Even when we are alone, we make use of our social knowledge to make sense of our lives, and we reflect on social events in which we have been involved. It is questionable whether anyone is truly independent, because the society and culture in which we live shape our thinking, and influence the choices we make.

Social psychologists have focused on a range of issues, varying in scope from detailed experimental examinations of non-verbal signalling, to large-scale surveys of the emergence of society-wide shared beliefs and social representations. Some social psychologists have explored social behaviour—how the presence of others affects what we do. Others have examined social cognition: how people make sense of social events and their role in them. As a consequence, research methods in social psychology range from detailed laboratory studies, involving precise measurement and rigid control over experimental variables, to interviewing people in everyday settings—or even in special ones, such as during strikes or religious gatherings.

One major controversy in social psychology concerns the shift towards obtaining socially meaningful data. Those advocating "traditional" approaches in social psychology have tended to measure only observed or observable behaviour, and to emphasise reliability of measurement—with the result that many aspects of social experience went unstudied. Proponents of the "new" approach tend to concentrate on the social meaning of events and ideas, and to emphasise that research should be valid and true to life. Thus, whereas the older research methods might involve measurement of distance, reaction time, or the number of correct or incorrect responses, new methods are based on finding out what someone thought about an event or experience, and the reasons he or she gave for why it happened. Of course, not all social psychology is this polarised. However, the two approaches to research are both current, and represent very different underlying views of the goals of research.

Another major issue that has emerged in recent years concerns the difference between European and American perspectives. An approach, often referred to as "European social psychology", has emerged within the past 20 years or so. This European approach tends to begin with theory building, so that research is mainly oriented towards the application, extension, or refutation of aspects of a given theory. In contrast, American social psychologists tend to begin by focusing on a particular type of event or problem, which they then attempt to explain. It is possible to make too much of this distinction, but the two approaches do represent genuinely different emphases in social psychological research.

The distinction between the American and European approaches can also be seen in the way in which modern social psychology responds to the broader social context. American social psychologists, like many British social psychologists until comparatively recently, generally examine social processes within the individual as if they were largely independent of anything except their immediate social context. In contrast, European social psychologists are much influenced by the contextual realities, including factors such as relative status, power, and ideology. Two of the most important "European" theories (*social representation theory* and *social identity theory*) are both firmly located in a world in which systematic social inequalities exist, and influence how people interact and what they come to believe.

As we have seen, contemporary social psychology encompasses a range of approaches and issues. It also encompasses a range of topics. An introductory study of social psychology is likely to include an examination of basic underlying social processes (such as non-verbal and verbal communication; ideas about the self; and concepts of social role and social norms). It will also include the study of what happens when people talk to one another—the analysis of discourse and of how people explain things, and of why some explanations are considered acceptable whereas others are not. Social psychology is also concerned with how we perceive others, why we find some people more attractive than others, and what happens as we develop relationships with them.

A major focus of modern social psychology is on issues of social conflict and co-operation. These issues range from inter-group conflict and prejudice, to crowd psychology, and to the altruism (unselfishness) that people often display towards others.

## Evaluation

Social psychology serves the valuable function of examining how we relate to other people and to the society in which we live. As we are social animals, social psychology potentially covers much that is of relevance to an understanding of human behaviour. It is noticeable that social psychologists have increasingly realised that potential, by studying the full range of issues relating to our social lives.

As with any approach, social psychology is limited in some ways. Until quite recently, there was a de-emphasis on the cognitive processes involved in social situations (e.g. the ways in which we interpret the behaviour of other people). It is still the case that biological and physiological factors which may influence our social behaviour are generally not investigated by social psychologists.

It is difficult to study social behaviour adequately because of its sheer complexity. Suppose, for example, we study social processes and behaviour within a small group of eight people. Among the factors influencing group behaviour are the inter-personal relationships among each possible pair within the group. There are 28 different pairs in a group of eight people, and of course a large number of three- and four-person groupings. In other words, there are so many factors determining the patterns of behaviour in such a group that it is likely to be extremely difficult to develop a detailed understanding of its underlying social dynamics.

# Developmental psychology

## Historical roots

It is generally accepted nowadays that it is important to study the psychology of childhood both for its own sake and because it helps us to understand adult thinking and behaviour. However, it was only when Sigmund Freud's (1856–1939) psychoanalytic theories became widely known earlier this century, that serious attention was paid to developmental psychology.

Freud claimed that conflicts and problems in early childhood could sow the seeds of adult neurosis. Recent evidence to support this claim has been obtained by George Brown. Questioning of 400 women in Islington revealed that 64% of those suffering from panic disorder and 39 % of those

Jean Piaget: 1896–1980 (circa 1925). From J.J. Ducret (1990). *Jean Piaget: Biographie et parcours intellectuel*, published by Editions Delachaux et Niestlé, Lausanne.

suffering from depression had experienced childhood adversity (e.g. parental indifference or abuse). In contrast, only 17% of those free from disorder had experienced childhood adversity.

The greatest impetus to developmental psychology came from the work of Jean Piaget (1896–1980). He spent several decades studying the development of thinking and intelligence through the years of childhood. In essence, he argued that children pass through several stages of cognitive development. The early stages are characterised by an exaggerated emphasis on perception, and on certain aspects of a situation to the exclusion of others. Young children are also egocentric, in that they take it for granted that their way of thinking about things is the only possible way. The last stage (that of formal operations) is reached at about the age of twelve, and involves the ability to think abstractly and to imagine what would happen in various hypothetical situations (e.g. when all the world's oil is used up). In a sentence, Piaget argued that cognitive development involves a shift from the irrational and the illogical to the rational and the logical.

Much of Piaget's early work involved the "clinical method"—children were asked questions in a relatively unstructured way, with Piaget trying to establish how much they understood of different problems. This approach was criticised for being unscientific, and Piaget and his fellow workers gradually became more precise in their experiments. However, it is generally agreed that he tended to present problems in ways which young children find difficult to understand. When essentially the same problems are presented in a more "user-friendly" fashion, children are much more successful at solving them (see Eysenck, 1984). In other words, Piaget tended fairly consistently to under-estimate the cognitive abilities of children of different ages.

## Current perspective

Contemporary developmental psychology owes a considerable debt to the pioneering efforts of Freud, Piaget, and others. However, its scope is much more wide-ranging, covering topics as diverse as attachment and separation, cognitive development, moral development, social development, and language acquisition.

An increased variety of research methods are used to study children's behaviour. Cognitive development is often assessed under laboratory conditions, whereas language acquisition can be studied by keeping a detailed record of children's use of language over a longish period of time. Social development can be assessed by taking video recordings of children interacting with others (e.g. their parents or other children), or simply by using observational methods (e.g. watching children in a playground).

One of the major issues in developmental psychology is whether adverse experiences in childhood have long-lasting negative effects stretching into adulthood. Freud argued that conflicts and traumas in childhood increased the chances of adult neurosis, and John Bowlby (1953) claimed that *maternal deprivation* (lack of a continuous, secure bond between mother and child) led to long-term damage to a child's social, intellectual, and emotional development. In addition, Freud and Bowlby both argued that the early years of life are especially important. According to Bowlby, a satisfactory relationship between mother and child is un-likely to develop if there is a lack of adequate mothering in its first year.

As we saw earlier in the chapter, adults suffering from a variety of mental disorders are much more likely than other adults to have had severely adverse childhoods. However, it is important to recognise that there have been relatively few studies investigating the possibility of *reversibility* (adverse experiences in childhood being reversed sub-sequently by remedial action). One such study was carried out by Davis (1976) on a girl called Isabelle. Her mother was a deaf-mute, and the two of them spent most of their time in a dark room cut off from other people. When Isabelle was discovered at the age of six, she made only a strange croaking sound. Her non-verbal intelligence and her social maturity were both less than those of a normal three-year-old child. However, as a result of loving care, she reached a normal educational level within two years. Even more surprisingly, she seemed to be very cheerful and energetic in spite of the appalling environment in which she had spent her early years.

There are several other cases demonstrating the existence of revers-ibility. As Clarke and Clarke (1976) concluded, "Early learning is mainly important for its foundational character. By itself, and when unrepeated over time, it serves as no more than a link in the developmental chain, shaping ... behaviour less and less powerfully as age increases".

## Evaluation

Almost all psychologists agree that developmental psychology has proved valuable in shedding light on adult behaviour, as well as revealing patterns of development. In spite of the phenomenon of reversibility, adult cognitive, social, and motivational behaviour is generally much influenced by the experiences and learning of childhood. Thus, the devel-opmental perspective is a crucial ingredient in working towards a com-plete understanding of adult functioning.

On the negative side, there are very real problems in carrying out experiments on infants and very young children. They cannot understand

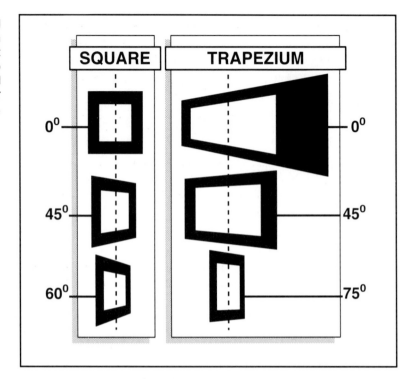

The square and trapezium presented at different slants to infants. Adapted from Slater (1989).

instructions, their attention wanders, and they cannot use language to describe their experience. However, developmental psychologists have been increasingly successful in overcoming these problems. Infants' perceptual abilities have been assessed by using a *habituation* procedure: infants spend less and less time looking at a visual stimulus which is presented repeatedly. For example, Slater and Morison (1985) presented newborns (average age two days) with a shape such as a square which changed in slant during the initial habituation stage. Subsequently, the newborns looked much more at a new shape (such as a trapezium) than at the old shape presented in a different orientation from any seen previously. This indicates that the old shape was perceived in some sense as being old in spite of looking different, suggesting that the basics of shape constancy are present at birth.

# Humanistic psychology

## Historical roots

During the nineteenth and early twentieth centuries, several philosophers including Jean-Paul Sartre in France, Soren Kierkegaard in Denmark, and

Martin Heidegger in Germany associated themselves with a position known as *existentialism*. The key aspects of existentialism were expressed in the following way by Ford and Urban (1963, p. 448):

> Man has the capacity for being aware of himself, of what he is doing, and what is happening to him. As a consequence, he is capable of making decisions about these things and of taking responsibility for himself … He does not exist; he is not a being; rather, he is coming into being, emerging, becoming, evolving towards something … His significance lies not in what he has been in the past, but in what he is now and the direction of his development, which is towards the fulfilment of his innate personality.

Thus, existentialism focuses on personal responsibility, free will, and the striving towards personal growth and fulfilment. This may sound as if existentialism is a positive and upbeat philosophical position. However, the existentialist philosophers also emphasised that the major choices we make in life are generally accompanied by anxiety.

Existentialist philosophers believed that we can understand others by focusing on their conscious experience. The notion that our conscious experience is of particular value was also an important part of the approach of the *Gestalt* psychologists (*Gestalt* is the German word for form or pattern). Gestalt psychology started around 1912, and involved three psychologists at the University of Frankfurt: Max Wertheimer, Kurt Koffka, and Wolfgang Kohler.

One of the main interests of the Gestalt psychologists lay in perception. They believed that the perceiver should describe his or her raw experience; a technique known as *phenomenology* (meaning the descriptive science of pure experience divested of all theoretical and practical implications). In contrast, several earlier psychologists had argued in favour of *analytical introspection*, in which the subject attempts to focus on specific parts of his or her experience.

## Current perspective

The *humanistic psychology* approach was developed primarily by Carl Rogers and Abraham Maslow, and came into prominence in the 1950s and 60s. In many ways, it applied the philosophical ideas of existentialism to psychology. According to Cartwright (1979), humanistic psychology "is concerned with topics that are meaningful to human beings, focusing especially upon subjective experience and the unique, unpredictable events in individual human lives" (pp. 5–6). More specifically, humanistic psychologists argue that psychology should be based on phenomenology.

Maslow (1954) pointed out that most psychologists interested in human motivation had focused on basic physiological needs, or on our needs to reduce anxiety and avoid pain. According to him, human motivation is actually much broader than that. Maslow proposed a *hierarchy of needs*. Physiological needs (such as those for food and water) are at the bottom of the hierarchy. Next come security and safety needs, followed by needs for love and belongingness. Moving further up the hierarchy, we come to esteem needs, then cognitive needs (such as curiosity and the need for understanding) and aesthetic (artistic) needs, and finally the need for self-actualisation.

All of the needs towards the bottom of the hierarchy were regarded as deficiency motivation, because they are designed to reduce inadequacies or deficiencies. In contrast, needs towards the top of the hierarchy (such as self-actualisation) represent growth motivation, and are designed to promote personal growth. Self-actualisation was described in the following way by Maslow (1954): "A musician must make music, an artist must

*Maslow's hierarchy of needs.*

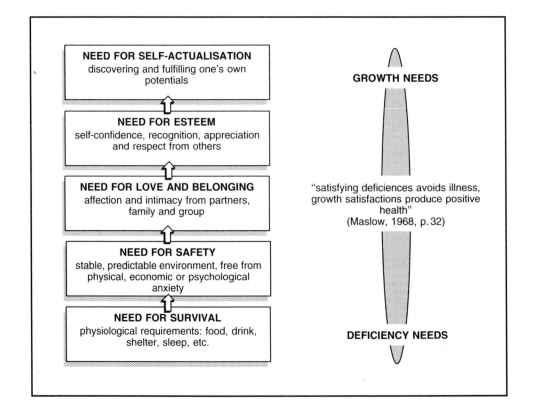

NEED FOR SELF-ACTUALISATION
discovering and fulfilling one's own potentials

NEED FOR ESTEEM
self-confidence, recognition, appreciation and respect from others

NEED FOR LOVE AND BELONGING
affection and intimacy from partners, family and group

NEED FOR SAFETY
stable, predictable environment, free from physical, economic or psychological anxiety

NEED FOR SURVIVAL
physiological requirements: food, drink, shelter, sleep, etc.

GROWTH NEEDS

"satisfying deficiences avoids illness, growth satisfactions produce positive health"
(Maslow, 1968, p. 32)

DEFICIENCY NEEDS

paint, a poet must write, if he is to be ultimately at peace with himself. What a man can be, he must be. This need we may call self-actualisation". Self-actualised individuals are characterised by an acceptance of themselves, spontaneity, the need for privacy, resistance to cultural influences, empathy, profound interpersonal relations, a democratic character structure, creativeness, and a philosophical sense of humour. Abraham Lincoln, Eleanor Roosevelt, and Albert Einstein were identified as famous people who were self-actualised.

Maslow (1962) attempted to study self-actualisation by focusing on *peak experiences*, in which the world is accepted completely for what it is, and there are feelings of euphoria, wonder, and awe. Peak experiences happen most frequently during sexual intercourse or when listening to music—and sometimes when doing both at the same time! Maslow assumed that self-actualised individuals would report more peak experiences than other people. Self-actualisation has also been assessed by means of self-report questionnaires such as the Index of Self-Actualisation.

One of the major assumptions made by Maslow was that the higher needs (such as the need for self-actualisation) will emerge only when lower needs (such as those for food and drink) are satisfied. Aronoff (1967) tested this assumption by comparing fishermen and cane cutters in the British West Indies. Fishermen worked on their own and generally earned more than cane cutters, who worked in groups and were paid on the basis of the amount of cane cut by the entire group. Cane cutting was a more secure job, because the rewards fluctuated much less than for fishermen, and because cane cutters were still paid even if they were unwell. It seems to follow from Maslow's theory that it would be mainly those whose security and esteem needs were met who would choose the more challenging and responsible job of fishermen. As predicted, only 25% of the fishermen had a high need for security or safety, against 80% of the cane cutters. In addition, 80% of the fishermen had high self-esteem, but only 20% of the cane cutters.

Probably the main impact of the humanistic approach has been on therapy, and Rogers' *client-centred therapy* is a good example of this. Rogers' starting point is that the concept of *self* is of fundamental importance, with our self-concept being based on our conscious experiences of ourselves and of our position in society. Individuals often experience problems and seek therapy when there is *incongruence* (a major discrepancy) between the self-concept and the ideal self—that is, between the way one actually is and the way one would like to be.

The essence of client-centred therapy is that the patient (or client in Rogers' terminology) discusses his or her self-concept and life goals with the therapist (called by Rogers the *facilitator*). The general intention is to create a comfortable atmosphere in which the client will share his or her experiences with the facilitator. The hope and expectation is that therapy will allow the client to develop increased self-esteem and reduce the discrepancy between his or her self-concept and ideal self, thus becoming better equipped to handle the problems of life.

Client-centred therapy has these characteristics because Rogers believed that people possess free will and are generally capable of making sensible decisions about their lives. Accordingly, what is required in therapy is a supportive environment. Thus, the therapist or facilitator should be unconditional in his or her positive regard for the client, and should be empathic (understanding the client's feelings).

## Evaluation

The humanistic approach has been successful in a number of ways. First, humanistic psychologists have consistently addressed issues of fundamental importance to human beings. They focus on the self-concept, on our most profound motivating forces, on our attempts to realise our potential as individuals, and so on. These issues are obviously more immediately relevant than most of the issues that have preoccupied more experimentally minded psychologists.

Second, the humanistic approach provides a more comprehensive theoretical framework for human motivation than is available in most other approaches (see Chapter 4). The fact that there are millions of people in Western society who feel extremely depressed and unfulfilled in spite of having all their basic physiological needs catered for suggests the importance of growth motivation.

Third, humanistic forms of therapy (such as client-centred therapy and encounter groups) have proved to be reasonably effective. However, the evidence suggests that they are more useful in the treatment of relatively mild disorders than of severe ones (Davison & Neale, 1990).

Fourth, humanistic psychology has forced many psychologists to question their basic beliefs. Humanistic psychologists differ from most other psychologists in focusing on conscious experience rather than behaviour; on free will rather than determinism; on understanding rather than prediction and control; and on discussion of experience rather than on use of the experimental method (see Chapter 3). Whether or not the views of humanistic psychologists are valid, they have certainly succeeded in injecting a breath of fresh air into psychology.

There are various criticisms that can be made of the humanistic approach. First, phenomenology is concerned only with those thoughts of which we have conscious awareness. As a consequence, it ignores all the important processes going on below the level of conscious awareness (see Chapter 3). Another problem with reliance on an individual's conscious experiences is that his or her report of those experiences may be systematically distorted (e.g. to create a good impression).

Second, the assumption that each individual is born with the potential to become a self-actualiser if his or her basic needs are met is dubious at best. The fact that a relatively small percentage of people are self-actualised does not prove that everyone could be. The main explanation for self-actualisation may simply be that self-actualised individuals tend to be much more intelligent, talented, well-educated, and motivated than the rest of us—in which case, most people probably could not become self-actualised. The fact that the average British person spends 25 hours a week watching television suggests that there are many people whose motivation for personal growth is not enormous!

Third, the notion that self-actualised individuals are creative, self-accepting, and have excellent interpersonal relations seems to lose sight of the fact that many individuals possess one of these characteristics but not the others. For example, the artist Van Gogh was outstandingly creative, but he was so lacking in self-acceptance that he committed suicide. There are numerous other examples of very creative individuals whose personal and emotional lives were disaster areas—should they be regarded as self-actualised or not?

Fourth, most humanistic psychologists argue that self-actualisation occurs primarily because of needs within the individual rather than because of the beneficial impact of the environment. Indeed, it is often claimed that society tends to impose conformity on people, and so makes it harder for individuals to become self-actualised. In fact, the environment often facilitates self-actualisation—most Western societies provide their citizens with many years of schooling, training opportunities for those exhibiting special skills, part-time courses, and so on. In other words, self-actualisation probably depends on external (environmental) as well as internal (need) factors, rather than almost entirely on internal ones.

Fifth, the humanistic rejection of the scientific approach to psychology involves some definite costs (see Chapter 5). Science tends to make progress over time, even if the rate is often disappointing. Thus, for example, many of the assumptions of the behaviourists have been discarded because they have been shown to be wrong. In contrast, there is much less sense of progress within the humanistic approach—its validity is not much clearer now than it was 40 years ago.

# Cognitive psychology

## Historical roots

The study of human cognition, with its focus on thinking and other mental processes, originated with Plato and Aristotle. It remained the dominant topic within psychology for approximately 2000 years, but was relatively ignored during the first half of the twentieth century because of the influence of behaviourism and its emphasis on behaviour rather than internal processes. John Watson, for example, argued "What the psychologists have hitherto called thought is nothing but talking to ourselves".

In contrast, cognitive psychologists focus mainly on the internal processes and structures involved in cognition (defined as "the mental act or process by which knowledge is acquired" in Collins *English Dictionary*), and so are interested in observable responses only to the extent that they provide information about these underlying processes and structures.

Cognitive psychology became of great importance in the mid-1950s. Several major factors were responsible for its rise. First, there was growing dissatisfaction with the behaviourist approach. It had become clear that an emphasis on behaviour rather than on internal processes was standing in the way of understanding cognitive abilities, such as our mastery of language or the processes involved in problem-solving.

Second, psychologists began to develop increasingly ingenious experimental tasks, which permitted much more accurate assessment of the internal processes being used by the subject. Consider, for example, the research on concept formation by Bruner, Goodnow, and Austin (1956). Subjects were presented with a large array of cards which varied on four dimensions: number of borders around the edges of the cards (one, two, or three); number of objects in the middle of the cards (one, two, or three); shape of the objects (square, circle, or cross); and colour of the objects (red, black, or green). The subjects had to select cards from the array one at a time, and after each choice the experimenter indicated whether it exemplified the concept. For example, if the concept was "two circles", then choosing the card with two red circles and one border would exemplify the concept, whereas choosing the card with two black squares and two borders would not. Bruner et al. examined carefully the patterns of choice made by subjects, which enabled them to work out the subjects' strategies.

Third, there was the advent of the "computer revolution". Psychologists have often attempted to understand the complexities of human cognition by comparing it with something simpler and better understood—catapults and telephone exchanges are among the numerous comparisons or analogies that have been used. There is fairly general agreement that the

"...SUFFERS THE OCCASIONAL BREAKDOWN, PRONE TO THE ODD VIRUS... I TELL YOU, THEY WERE MADE FOR EACH OTHER..."

*computer analogy* provides a more realistic basis for understanding human cognition than previous comparisons. Computers share some of the complexities of the human brain, and resemble our brains in having inputs and outputs, memory stores, and active processing systems. In addition, they possess flexibility.

We have already discussed most of the major factors lying behind the emergence of cognitive psychology. A final (largely unsung) influence was that of neurologists such as Carl Wernicke and Paul Broca. Towards the end of the nineteenth century, Wernicke discovered that patients with damage to an area of the brain that came to be called *Wernicke's area* had a severe impairment of the ability to comprehend spoken and written language, but could speak reasonably normally (Wernicke, 1874).

This work had been preceded by that of Paul Broca (1865). He found some brain-damaged patients had great difficulty with speaking, but their comprehension of language was normal. These patients had all suffered damage to what is known as *Broca's speech area*.

This early work was largely ignored by psychologists for several decades. However, interest in studying brain-damaged patients in order to discover more about human cognition has revived tremendously, as we will see shortly.

## Current perspective

As Eysenck and Keane (1990) pointed out, there are three main strands in contemporary cognitive psychology: *experimental cognitive psychology, cognitive science,* and *cognitive neuropsychology*. Experimental cognitive psychology is based largely on laboratory-based studies of cognition in normal individuals, and as such closely resembles the traditional approach of the past 40 years. In contrast, cognitive science and cognitive neuropsychology are more recent developments, and deserve fuller consideration.

An important aspect of cognitive science is the attempt to produce computer programs that will mimic the processes and outputs of the human brain. One advantage of this approach over experimental cognitive psychology is that full details of how a cognitive task is to be performed must be spelled out in the computer program, whereas the traditional verbal accounts provided by cognitive psychologists often gloss over important points. The cognitive science approach has also been in the forefront of theoretical progress in recent years. Most theories in cognitive psychology have been based on the assumption that cognitive processes occur in a serial fashion (one at a time, in other words), in spite of the fact that the brain appears to function as a parallel processing system (handling more than one thing at a time). Some cognitive scientists have responded to this challenge by producing *parallel distributed processing* theories, which seem more in accord with the actual functioning of the brain .

Cognitive neuropsychologists study cognitive processes in brain-damaged patients. However, they have provided much useful information about the workings of the cognitive system in normal individuals. For example, the fact that some brain-damaged patients can remember things for a few seconds but not over long periods of time, whereas others have relatively good memory over long but not short periods, provides strong support for the theory that normal people possess separate short-term and long-term memory systems.

One of the most impressive features of cognitive psychology has been its penetration of several other areas of psychology. For example, many developmental psychologists approach human development from the cognitive perspective. Jean Piaget (1896–1980) was primarily interested in the successive stages of cognitive development through which children pass on their way to adulthood. In similar fashion, the cognitive approach has become influential in areas such as social and clinical psychology.

## Evaluation

The approach of cognitive psychology, and the experimental techniques used by cognitive psychologists, have led to a much fuller understanding of the processes and structures involved in human cognition. Human language, for example, which had been almost totally ignored by the behaviourists, has been studied with great thoroughness by cognitive psychologists.

Cognitive psychology has been greatly strengthened by the way in which important issues are being tackled by means of traditional experimental research, studies on brain-damaged patients, and computer simulations. In general terms, looking at an issue from three different angles makes it much easier to understand than if it were looked at from a single perspective.

On the negative side, there are legitimate doubts about the ultimate value of the computer analogy. There are usually several different ongoing processes in the human brain at any given time, and human thinking tends to be somewhat imprecise, because we find it difficult to bear several different pieces of information in mind at once. In contrast, until relatively recently, most computer programs permitted only one process to occur at a time, and computer functioning is typically very precise. Even more importantly, there may be absolutely fundamental differences between computers and humans. As the philosopher A.J. Ayer pointed out, it is difficult to "allow machines an inner life, to credit them with feeling and emotion, to treat them as moral agents".

Another problem with cognitive psychology is that much of the research and theorising is rather specific—we have theories of attention, of perception, of learning, and of memory. What we don't have are many general theories that integrate the different parts of cognitive psychology into a coherent whole.

# General conclusions

Eleven different approaches have been discussed in this chapter. The historical roots of each approach have been dealt with separately, but in reality the historical development of psychology was more complex than has been indicated so far. An attempt to provide a more realistic description of the major influences on current perspectives to psychology is shown in the chart on page 57.

One of the interesting features of the chart is that it helps to clarify why it is that certain individuals and approaches have been so important in the development of psychology. For example, Charles Darwin had an impact in various different ways: he influenced contemporary comparative psychology via the ethologists; he influenced the individual differences approach via Francis Galton; and he influenced behaviourism. In turn, behaviourism has played a role in the development of comparative psychology, abnormal psychology (in the form of behaviour therapy), and cognitive psychology (in the form of rigorous scientific procedures).

Another feature is that there is some evidence of a pattern. In general, the starting point for many areas of psychology was a dominant individual (such as Darwin or Freud), usually during the nineteenth century. In the early part of the twentieth century, the focus shifted away from individuals and towards specific new disciplines which began to emerge (such as ethology or psychometrics). Finally, the combined influence of these key individuals and these emerging disciplines helped to establish the major areas of psychology we see today.

The chart opposite is designed to give an indication of the present situation in psychology, and to show some of the main factors which have led to that situation. However, what it does not show clearly is that there are important inter-connections among most of the main areas of psychology. For example, there are links between social psychology and cognitive psychology because many social psychologists study social cognition (cognitive processes in social situations); there are links between abnormal psychology and psychophysiology because physiological measures are often taken from clinical patients; and there are links between comparative psychology and developmental psychology because some comparative psychologists focus on the process of development in non-human species.

The fact that there signs of integration across the main areas of psychology is potentially valuable. Although each perspective is valuable in its own right, a complete understanding of human behaviour can probably only be obtained by combining the knowledge and insights of each area into a fully integrated approach.

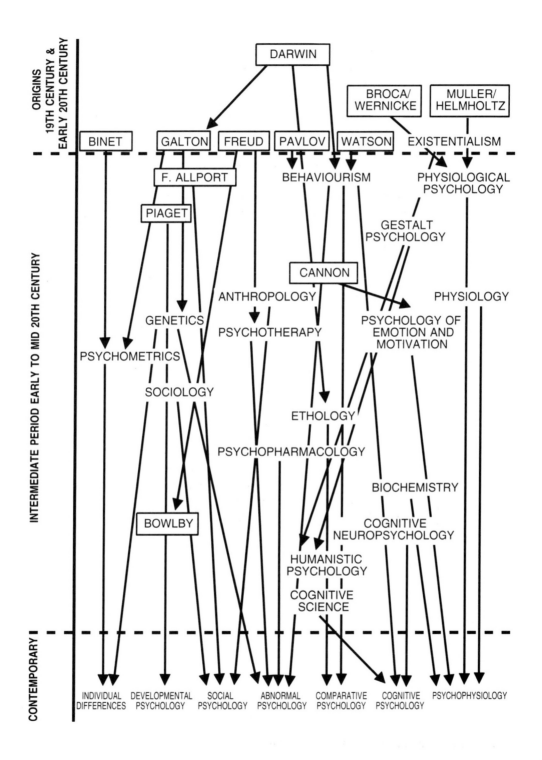

# Summary

- Psychology has been enriched by developments in numerous other disciplines, including physiology, neurology, sociology, zoology, anthropology, and biology.
- Sigmund Freud originated *psychoanalysis*, which is both a complex set of theories and a form of therapy.
- Psychoanalysis as a therapy was the first systematic attempt to treat clinical patients in a specifically psychological fashion.
- Psychoanalysis was probably the first reasonably effective treatment for neurosis, but its success depends only partially on the theoretical ideas put forward by Freud.
- Behaviourism consisted of two main components: (1) assumptions about the methods to be used in psychology (such as an emphasis on behaviour); and (2) a theory of learning and behaviour.
- The behaviourists' insistence on careful observation of behaviour and on the use of the experimental method remains influential, but their theory of behaviour is now of marginal importance.
- The development of *abnormal psychology* was much influenced by psychoanalysis (which led to various other forms of psychotherapy), by behaviourism (which led to behaviour therapy), and by the introduction of bodily manipulations such as electroconvulsive shock therapy and drug treatments.
- Contemporary forms of treatment include cognitive therapy, modified versions of behaviour therapy, and somatic therapy (largely based on drugs); most of these therapies seem to be comparable in effectiveness.
- The *biological* approach to psychology started with Darwin; it emphasises the value of studying other species (*comparative psychology*), heredity, and individual differences.
- The biological approach led to *human sociobiology*, according to which we try to maximise the number of descendants of ourselves and of our families; the development of knowledge and culture has greatly reduced its applicability.
- One of the most important approaches within comparative psychology is *ethology*, in which non-human species are studied in their natural habitat.
- The similarities between the human species and others are greater for activities depending on the reptile brain and the paleocortex than those depending on the neocortex.
- Over the past 150 years, *physiological psychology* has contributed much to our understanding of perception.

- Recent technological advances (such as positron emission tomography) allow us to identify relatively precisely those parts of the brain that are most active during the performance of any given task.
- Much work within the *individual differences* approach has focused on intelligence and personality; their structure has been investigated by a combination of psychometrics and factor analysis.
- Intelligence and personality are often regarded as stable over time, but many individuals show significant changes in both characteristics.
- There has been a shift in *social psychology* towards the study of the social meaning of events and ideas, and the importance of ecological validity is increasingly accepted.
- The emergence of *developmental psychology* owes much to the influence of Sigmund Freud and Jean Piaget.
- Many of the detrimental effects of childhood adversity are reversible if remedial help is provided.
- Humanistic psychology has its roots in existentialism and phenomenology.
- Two of the main achievements of humanistic psychology are Maslow's theory of motivation based on a hierarchy of needs and Rogers' client-centred therapy.
- The anti-scientific stance of humanistic psychologists means that their theories are difficult to test properly.
- Cognitive psychology consists of three main strands: experimental cognitive psychology, cognitive science, and cognitive neuropsychology.
- Relatively few general theories have emerged from cognitive psychology.

## Further reading

For further reading, the major approaches within psychology are discussed by A.M. Colman in *What is psychology? The inside story* (London, Hutchinson, 1988). Good accounts of the history of psychology are to be found in *The shaping of modern psychology: An historical introduction* by L. Hearnshaw (London, Routledge & Kegan Paul, 1987), and *Historical introduction to modern psychology* by G. Murphy and J.K. Kovach (London, Routledge & Kegan Paul, 1972).

# 3

# Major issues in psychology

Several rather broad issues are of importance to the study of psychology: some are essentially philosophical (such as free will versus determinism); whereas others are theoretical (idiographic versus nomothetic explanations, or the value of introspection). Still others (such as nature versus nurture or consciousness) are both theoretical and philosophical. The common factor is a relevance to the nature of the psychological discipline. Much controversy has surrounded some of these issues in the past, and still does to a lesser extent; but there is now a fair measure of agreement among psychologists on their attitudes to most of the topics discussed in this chapter.

It is probably true to say that psychology has been faced by more controversy about its basic nature than is the case with other scientific disciplines. Why should this be so?

In part, it reflects the complexity of psychology. In physics, one piece of a metal may closely resemble another piece of the same metal, and in chemistry two instances of the same chemical element are very similar to each other. In psychology, however, each individual is unique, which greatly complicates the task of uncovering general principles that are applicable to everyone.

Another unusual feature of psychology, of course, is the fact that its researchers belong to the same species as the one they are studying. Apart from anything else, this means psychologists (like the rest of the human race) are likely to have various preconceptions about human behaviour which colour their approach to research. The fact that psychologists have a variety of preconceptions helps to account for some of the controversies. In contrast, chemists presumably do not have strong, irrational feelings about the nature of the chemical elements with which they have to deal!

"SO WE ALL AGREE GENTLEMEN; THAT EVERYBODY IS UNIQUE."

# Reductionism

According to the *Concise Oxford Dictionary*, reductionism can be defined as "the analysis of complex things into simple constituents". Within the context of psychology, the term has been used to refer to two somewhat different theoretical approaches.

The first involves the belief that the phenomena of psychology can potentially be accounted for within the framework of more basic sciences or disciplines (such as physiology). The second approach is based on the assumption that complex forms of behaviour can be explained in terms of simple principles. For example, as we saw in Chapter 1, many association-ists believed that complicated human thought processes occur as a result of the association of ideas.

## Psychology as a scientific discipline

Psychology is obviously related to several other scientific disciplines: it involves attempting to understand people's (and other species') behaviour, and this is determined in part by basic internal processes of interest to biochemists and physiologists. As people are social animals, their behaviour is also influenced by a variety of social processes (such as conformity, and the desire to impress others). The multi-disciplinary nature of psychology has led many psychologists to focus on the important issue of the way in which their subject is related to other sciences.

It is possible to think of different scientific disciplines as being organised in a hierarchical fashion, with the less precise and more general sciences at the top, and the more precise and narrowly focused sciences at the bottom. For example, one could construct a hierarchy including psychology which might look like this:

1. *Sociology*: the science of groups and societies.
2. *Psychology*: the science of human and animal behaviour and its explanation.
3. *Physiology*: the science of functional working of the healthy body.
4. *Biochemistry*: the science of the chemistry of living organisms.

It has been argued by reductionists that the sciences towards the top of the hierarchy will ultimately be replaced by those towards the bottom. In the case of psychology, this implies that it should be possible one day to explain psychological phenomena in physiological or biochemical terms.

There is no doubt this theory has an immediate appeal. Biochemistry, physiology, psychology, and sociology are all concerned with human functioning, so there is some overlap in their subject matter. There is also a sense in which biochemistry and physiology are more developed and "scientific" than psychology and sociology. Accordingly, there would appear to be grounds for preferring biochemical or physiological explanations of behaviour to those offered by psychology.

However, there are strong arguments against this kind of reductionism. As Putnam (1973) pointed out, much human behaviour cannot be understood solely in terms of basic biological and physiological processes: "Psychology is as under-determined by biology as it is by elementary particle physics, and ... people's psychology is partly a reflection of deeply entrenched societal beliefs" (p. 141).

Putnam's general position can be illustrated by considering a simple example. Suppose a psychologist wants to predict how a group of people will vote in a forthcoming election. No-one in their right mind would argue that a detailed biochemical and physiological examination of their brains would be very informative! Voting behaviour is obviously determined by social attitudes, group pressures, and so on, rather than directly by underlying biochemical and physiological processes.

However, it is reasonable to assume that at least some issues within psychology do lend themselves to the reductionist perspective. This suggests the usefulness of the reductionist approach may depend very much on the specific questions we are asking.

## Reducing complex issues to simple parts

Reductionism is also involved when theorists attempt to reduce complex phenomena to separate simple parts: a clear example is B.F. Skinner's (1957) explanation of the acquisition of language, suggesting children master linguistic complexities primarily because their language responses are rewarded or reinforced. This is certainly a very reductionist approach, but the evidence indicates strongly that language acquisition cannot be accounted for in such simple terms (see Chomsky, 1959). In similar fashion, the reductionist proposal that thinking consists solely of chains of associated ideas is manifestly inadequate (see Hearnshaw, 1987).

Some of the problems associated with the reductionist position can be seen if we consider the chemistry of water ($H_2O$): it is possible to reduce water to hydrogen (H) and oxygen (O). Hydrogen burns and oxygen is necessary for burning, whereas water lacks both of those attributes. Here is a case where a reductionist approach may confuse rather than clarify.

In general terms, phenomena in psychology are usually better explained in terms of various factors operating at different levels of complexity, rather than in terms of a number of factors at a low level of complexity. For example, a complete account of children's acquisition of language requires the combined expertise of developmental, social, and cognitive psychologists, as well as psycholinguists.

In sum, we have seen that there is little evidence to support a thoroughgoing reductionist position. However, it is important to note that reductionism is not a theory in the sense of generating testable hypotheses; instead, it provides a set of assumptions which can be used to guide the theory and research produced by psychologists. As such, it is difficult to know whether or not reductionism may prove to be of future value, although the omens at present do not look favourable.

## Alternatives to reductionism

Humanistic psychology provides one alternative to reductionism, based essentially on ignoring reductionism altogether. Theorists such as Rogers attach great significance to the self-concept (our perception of ourselves and our position in the world) and to the efforts of humans to realise their potential by means of self-actualisation. They argue that the self should be investigated by asking people to provide reports of their conscious experiences, because this provides the most direct evidence of how the self functions. Within this approach, there is no systematic attempt to divide the self up into smaller units, or to identify the physiological processes associated with the self.

The humanistic approach is rather limited in some ways. The refusal to consider any kind of reductionism suggests that humanistic psychologists do not believe that physiological and biological factors are of any real significance. Each individual's conscious experience may be of importance in understanding his or her behaviour, but it seems improbable that no other factors need to be taken into account.

Another alternative to reductionism is what one might call the eclectic approach, in which relevant information is gathered together from various different sources and disciplines. Consider, for example, the scientific issue of discovering the causes of schizophrenia (a serious condition involving hallucinations and loss of contact with reality). There is evidence that genetic factors are involved, and at the biochemical level some studies have suggested that schizophrenics tend to be unduly sensitive to the neurotransmitter dopamine (see Davison & Neale, 1990). Other evidence reviewed by Davison and Neale suggests that poor social relationships and adverse life events also play a part in producing schizophrenia.

In the light of the evidence on schizophrenia, reductionists might be tempted to produce a biochemical theory of schizophrenia. However, such an approach would de-emphasise environmental factors such as life events. According to the eclectic approach, a full understanding of schizophrenia will necessitate considering all the relevant factors and the ways in which they combine together.

The major problem with the eclectic approach is that it is very difficult to integrate information from different disciplines into a single theory. For example, it is not immediately clear how the concepts and terminology of biochemistry can be combined with those of life event research. In spite of this problem, it seems likely that psychology should not ignore potentially valuable information from other disciplines.

## Free will versus determinism

The issue of free will versus determinism has occupied philosophers and psychologists over the centuries. The central question was expressed by Henry Sidgwick (quoted by John Mabbott, 1954, p. 746):

> Is my voluntary action at any moment completely determined by (1) my character as it has been partly inherited, partly formed by my past actions and feelings, and (2) my circumstances, or the external influences acting on me at the moment? Or not? Could the volition [wish] I am just about to originate be certainly calculated by anyone who knew my

character at this moment and the forces acting upon me? Or is there a strictly incalculable element in it?

In essence, advocates of determinism claim that people's actions are totally determined by the external and internal forces operating on them. Advocates of free will argue that matters are more complicated, and that there is an "incalculable element" involved.

" TO BE..."     "OR NOT TO BE..."   "THAT IS THE QUESTION."

The distinction between free will and determinism can be seen if we consider the following question: "Could an individual's behaviour in a given situation have been different if he or she had so willed it?" Most believers in free will would answer that question, "Yes", whereas most advocates of determinism would respond, "No".

## Determinism

Determinists have often claimed a proper science of human behaviour is possible only if one adopts a deterministic viewpoint: assuming simply that everything which happens has a definite cause. If this is disputed, and an "incalculable element" is taken into account, it becomes impossible to predict human behaviour with any precision. With other sciences, it is sometimes possible to make very accurate predictions from a deterministic position (forecasts of planetary motion, for example). If determinism is deemed not to be applicable to psychology, then psychology is either a very different science to physics, chemistry, and so on, or it is not a science at all.

These determinist arguments have been weakened somewhat by the progress of science in the twentieth century. It is increasingly recognised that precise prediction based on an understanding of the causal factors involved is the exception rather than the rule, even in sciences such as physics and chemistry. For example, according to the "principle of indeterminacy", it is impossible to determine the position and movement of an electron at the same time.

Most psychologists believe in determinism rather than free will, but the behaviourists held this belief especially strongly. Skinner, for example, was very unwilling to accept that internal processes influence the way we behave. He argued instead that virtually all our behaviour is determined by environmental factors (e.g. we repeat behaviour that has been rewarded and don't repeat behaviour that has not been rewarded).

Many psychologists favour a position known as *soft determinism*, a term introduced into psychology by William James. According to this position, we can distinguish between behaviour that is highly constrained by the situation (and thus appears involuntary) and behaviour that is only modestly constrained by the situation (and thus appears voluntary). For example, a child may apologise for swearing either because he or she is threatened with punishment if an apology is not forthcoming (highly constrained behaviour) or because he or she is genuinely upset at causing offence (modestly constrained behaviour). Behaviour is determined in either case, but the underlying causes are more obvious when it is highly constrained by situational forces.

The main problem with determinism (whether soft or not) is that it is not really possible to submit it to proper test. If all behaviour is determined by internal and external forces, then in theory it should be possible to predict behaviour from a knowledge of these causal factors. In fact, as we have seen, predictability is very often not possible in other sciences, and has proved very elusive in psychology. It is thus no more than an article of faith that human behaviour can eventually be predicted accurately.

## Free will

Most people have the subjective impression that they possess free will, in the sense that they can freely choose what to do from a number of possibilities. As Dr Samuel Johnson said to Boswell, "We know our will is free, and there's an end on't". Most people also have feelings of personal responsibility, presumably because they feel that they are in at least partial control of their behaviour.

Humanistic psychologists such as Carl Rogers and Abraham Maslow (see Chapter 2) are among those who believe in free will. Rogers' client-centred therapy is based on the assumption that the client has free will. The therapist is called a "facilitator" precisely because his or her role is to make it easier for the client to exercise free will in such a way as to maximise the rewardingness of the client's life. Going along with the belief in free will, most humanistic psychologists are more or less opposed to the scientific approach. They argue that regarding human behaviour as being determined by external forces is "de-humanising" and incorrect.

Those who support the notion of free will have to face up to at least two major problems. First, it is rather difficult to provide a precise account of what is meant by free will. As determinism is based on the assumption that all behaviour is caused, it could be argued that free will implies that behaviour is uncaused or random. However, very few people would want to argue for such a position—anyone whose behaviour appeared random would probably be classified as mentally ill or very stupid! If free will does not imply that behaviour is uncaused, then we need to know how free will plays a part in causing behaviour.

Second, there is the difficulty that most successful sciences are based on the assumption of determinism. It is possible, of course, that determinism applies to the natural world but does not apply to humans. If that is the case, then there are enormous implications for psychology which have hardly been addressed as yet.

## Conclusions

The issue of free will versus determinism has generated more heat than light for a number of reasons. First, it is not clear that it makes much sense to talk about "free will", because this presupposes there is an agent (i.e. the will) which may or may not operate in an unfettered fashion. As the philosopher John Locke pointed out, "We may as properly say that the singing faculty sings and the dancing faculty dances as that the will chooses".

Second, the issue is essentially philosophical rather than scientific: it is impossible to design an experiment to decide whether or not free will influences human behaviour. As William James (1890) expressed it, "the fact is that the question of free will is insoluble on strictly psychological grounds" (p. 323). In other words, we can never know whether an individual's behaviour in a particular situation could have been different if he or she had so willed it.

Third, although those who believe in determinism or free will often appear to have totally irreconcilable views, there may well be more common ground between them than is generally realised. Regardless of their position on the issue, nearly all psychologists accept that heredity, past experience, and the present environment all influence our behaviour. Although some of these factors (such as the environment) are external to the individual, others are internal; and most of these internal factors (such as character or personality) are the results of causal sequences stretching back into the past. The dispute then narrows to the issue of whether a solitary internal factor—variously called free will or self—is somehow immune from the influence of the past.

Fourth, and perhaps most important, we can go a step further and see that there is no necessary incompatibility between determinism and free will at all. According to determinists, it is possible in principle to demonstrate that an individual's actions are caused by a sequence of physical activities in the brain. If free will (e.g. conscious thinking and deciding) forms part of that sequence, it is possible to believe in free will and human responsibility at the same time as holding to a deterministic position. This would not be the case if free will is regarded as an intruder forcing its way into the sequence of physical activities in the brain, but there are no good grounds for adopting this position. In other words, the entire controversy between determinism and free will may be artificial and of less concern to psychologists than has been thought.

## Nature versus nurture

Even the most casual observation of other people reveals enormous individual differences in personality, intelligence, and other personal characteristics; and psychologists have devoted much attention to the issue of why people differ so much from each other.

At the most general level, there are only two possible reasons for individual differences: heredity, or *nature*; and environment, or *nurture*. In other words, people differ either because of differences in the genetic potential they have inherited, or because of differences in the environment or circumstances they have encountered. In fact, it is highly probable that nature and nurture both play a part in producing individual differences.

Those who believe nurture is of overwhelming importance are known as *empiricists*, and include among their number most behaviourists and the followers of Sigmund Freud. Those who emphasise the role of nature in determining behaviour are known as *nativists*. The Gestaltist psychologists from Germany, some intelligence and personality theorists (such as Burt, H.J. Eysenck, Galton, and Spearman), and the ethologists (those studying animal behaviour from a zoological perspective) may all be regarded as nativists.

The nature–nurture issue can be expressed in a more precise fashion using two technical terms to describe what makes up a human being:

- genotype: the individual's genetic potential;
- phenotype: the individual's observable characteristics, including physical characteristics such as height and hair colour.

Psychologists are primarily interested in the *behavioural phenotype*, which is the pattern of behaviour shown by each individual, but in the sense of general and habitual characteristics of behaviour rather than specific responses. General behavioural characteristics are more meaningful than individual responses—it would be easier to decide whether someone was an anxious person, for example, if we observed their behaviour across several different situations rather than on just one occasion.

A crucial question is whether or not *genotypic* differences within a sample of individuals are predictive of individual differences in behavioural phenotypes. In other words, does the genetic potential represented by the genotype have a significant influence on the behavioural phenotype? If the answer is "yes", the next issue is to consider the relative contributions of heredity and environment to individual differences in behaviour. It is also important (although more so for behaviour geneticists than for psychologists) to investigate in detail the genetic mechanisms responsible for producing a link between the genotype and the phenotype.

The nature–nurture issue has been the source of much controversy. Some psychologists argue that investigating the role of heredity in determining individual differences in the behavioural phenotype can be unethical. Far and away the best known example of ethically problematic nature–nurture research relates to race differences in intelligence in the United States.

The tested intelligence of white Americans is generally higher than that of black Americans, but the proper interpretation of this difference has been hotly disputed. Jensen (1969) argued that intelligence depends heavily on heredity, and most of the difference in measured intelligence or intelligence quotient (IQ) is due to race differences in genetic endowment. Because Jensen's conclusions could be regarded as supporting the view that some races are "superior" to others, there was an immediate furore. It was pointed out that black Americans tend to be culturally deprived relative to white Americans, so their lower IQ scores could stem from environmental rather than hereditary factors. Whatever the rights and wrongs of Jensen's position, it is certainly true that the publicity his views received caused damage to race relations in America.

In fact, it is quite impossible on the basis of the evidence to reach any definite conclusion. We do not have detailed information of genotypic differences between white and black Americans, nor do we have detailed information about any environmental differences between the two groups. In such circumstances, and given the adverse effects on race relations that have occurred, research on racial differences in intelligence is very difficult to defend.

Some psychologists have argued that no research on humans has told us anything about the relative contributions of nature and nurture to behaviour, because of inherent research problems. In terms of nature or heredity, it is impossible to manipulate genotypic differences through selective breeding, nor can genotypic differences between individuals be controlled or manipulated in more than a very minor way. Furthermore, it is not usually even clear which aspects of the environment are most likely to affect the behavioural phenotype in question. In other words, the normal experimental method (see Chapter 5), in which the independent variable is systematically manipulated to observe its effects on the dependent variable (such as behaviour), cannot be used to investigate the nature–nurture issue.

A further difficulty with disentangling the effects of nature and nurture is that heredity and environment tend to be correlated—favourable heredity is found with favourable environment, and unfavourable heredity with unfavourable environment. For example, Galton (1869) discovered that close relatives of eminent or famous men were much more likely to achieve eminence than more distant relatives or a random sample of the population. Galton argued that this occurred because close relatives of eminent men usually inherit the genes for high intellectual ability. However, it is equally likely that they are brought up in a stimulating environment which facilitates the achievement of eminence.

There is, however, an inescapable limitation of research in this area. We cannot make sensible statements about the relative contributions of heredity and environment in any given individual. Instead, we are at best limited to conclusions about the role of heredity and environment in a specified population at a given point in time. It is also important to understand that the behavioural phenotype invariably depends on both the genotype and the environment. If either the appropriate genotype or the appropriate environment is missing, there can be no behavioural phenotype.

## The way ahead

Probably the best way to make progress is to stop thinking of heredity and environment in general terms, and to focus on different kinds of hereditary and environmental influence. So far as the environment is concerned, Lerner (1986) identified a number of different levels of the environment:

- inner-biological level—physiological influences on the unborn child;
- inner-psychological level—psychological influences of the mother

on the unborn child;

- physical-environmental level—effects of the physical environment (such as lead poisoning and pollution) on the child;
- sociocultural level—current knowledge and practices in education, recreation, and so on, which can affect children's development.

So far as hereditary influences are concerned, these can vary substantially in terms of how directly they affect behaviour. For example, there are very powerful effects of heredity in a condition known as *Down's syndrome*, in which babies are born with 47 chromosomes instead of the normal 46. Children with Down's syndrome generally suffer from moderate mental retardation, and their build is short and stocky. At present, these effects cannot be reversed by environmental manipulations.

Another condition caused by hereditary factors is phenylketonuria (PKU). Infants with PKU lack an exzyme that metabolises phenylalanine (a constituent of many foods, especially dairy products). Phenylalanine can build up in the body to dangerous levels, leading to profound mental retardation. Although the condition is produced by genetic factors, it differs from Down's syndrome in that some environmental remedial treatment is possible. If infants with PKU are given a diet low in phenylalanine, then their cognitive development is much better than it would be otherwise. Here is a clear example of increasing medical knowledge allowing environmental factors to reduce the negative effects of heredity.

As Malim, Birch, and Wadeley (1992) pointed out, there are other hereditary defects which can be alleviated by providing the appropriate kind of environment. Deafness and blindness are examples of hereditary defects which make life more difficult, but whose negative effects can be alleviated by providing the right environment.

Hereditary influences which are more indirect than any of those we have considered so far are those for various physical diseases. For example, there is evidence that heart disease tends to run in families, but susceptibility to heart disease can be counteracted by having a less stressful and more healthy life style (taking exercise regularly, avoiding foods high in cholesterol, and so on).

In sum, there are many different kinds of environmental and hereditary influences on human behaviour, and these influences differ in terms of how powerfully and directly they affect human behaviour. It is much more fruitful to identify specific genetic and environmental influences on behaviour rather than to focus on general (and unanswerable) questions such as, "Is nature or nurture more important?".

# Idiographic versus nomothetic approaches

The controversy between idiographic and nomothetic approaches raises fundamental issues about the nature and purpose of psychology. The terms were invented by Windelband in the nineteenth century, but were introduced into psychology by Gordon Allport (1937). They are based on two Greek words: *idios* meaning own or private, and *nomos* meaning law. The *idiographic* approach emphasises the uniqueness of every individual and argues that psychology should focus on individuals and their personal histories. By contrast, the *nomothetic* approach is based on the assumption that psychology is a science which seeks general laws of human behaviour, even if this is achieved at the expense of a detailed understanding of individuals.

## The idiographic approach

Those of an idiographic persuasion argue that no two individuals are the same, because everyone differs in terms of their heredity and particular sequences of experiences. As a consequence, what is true of one individual is by no means necessarily true of another, so the use of group data, combining information from several different unique individuals, cannot be recommended. Instead, each individual should be studied in detail over a longish period of time (known as a *longitudinal study*).

A case study reported by Allport (1965) can be used to illustrate the idiographic approach. He made use of approximately 300 letters written by a woman called "Jenny" over a period of several years. Detailed examination of these letters revealed the existence of various recurrent major themes, and allowed Allport to form an impression of Jenny's personality.

The idiographic approach clearly falls foul of the Latin saying, *Scientia non est individuorum* (Science does not deal with individual cases). Furthermore, it relies heavily on case studies, the use of biographical information, and relatively unstructured methods such as open-ended interviews; and by its very nature statistical analysis is generally inappropriate. However, Allport (1937) claimed the idiographic approach could actually be more scientific than nomothetism: "Psychology will become *more* scientific, i.e. better able to make predictions, when it has learned how to tell what will happen to *this* child's IQ if we change his environment in a certain way". There may be some substance in Allport's argument, but there is clearly more to science than making accurate predictions of a single individual's performance.

It is possible to take account of individual differences while remaining scientific by assuming that all individuals can be placed at some point on each of a set of personality dimensions (such as introversion–extraversion, or trait anxiety). This approach accepts that individuals differ from each other, but also accepts that individuals who are similar in personality (such as anxious introverts) can be grouped together for certain purposes.

This approach doesn't recommend itself to Allport or other idiographic psychologists, who claim that every person is absolutely unique. According to them, even if two people are very similar in terms of a particular personality trait (such as sociability), the way in which the trait is manifested in behaviour will depend on its relationship with other traits (such as aggressiveness); and it is thus impossible to make accurate predictions of behaviour on the basis of measures of isolated traits. In addition, personality traits are no more than artificial abstractions from reality, and so are of little use. The apparent conclusion from these arguments is that each person's uniqueness makes a true scientific approach to personality impossible.

There is some validity in most of the arguments put forward by idiographic psychologists, but some believe they have drawn the wrong conclusion from the uniqueness of human personality. This can perhaps be seen if we consider individual differences in age. If we measured everyone's age to the nearest hundredth of a second, it is highly probable every person on this planet is entirely unique in terms of his or her current age. However, it would seem strange to use that fact to deny any value in classifying individuals in terms of how old they are!

If everyone is unique, then people differ from each other in several ways. However, the existence of differences implies the existence of similarities, and there is every reason for supposing that these differences and similarities occur with respect to various dimensions of personality. For example, Jane and Peter are similar in terms of how extraverted they are, but differ considerably in their anxiety levels. As Guilford (1936) pointed out, many psychologists "seem unable to see that one individual can differ quantitatively from another in many variables, common variables though they may be, and still have a unique personality" (p. 675). In other words, uniqueness *can* be handled within a scientific approach to individual differences.

A strict application of the idiographic approach seems to imply that each person has his or her own unique personality traits (personality characteristics). As Brody (1988) has pointed out, this leads to a ludicrous position: "If the trait applies to only one person, then it cannot be described in terms that apply to more than one person. This would require one to invent a new language to describe each person or, perhaps, to develop the skills of a poet to describe an individual" (p. 110).

In sum, the idiographic approach can provide a detailed and thorough understanding of a given individual. However, for many purposes this is simply not enough. As Holt (1967, p. 397) concluded:

> No matter how intensively prolonged, objective and well-controlled the study of a single case, one can never be sure to what extent the lawful regularities found can be generalised to other persons, or in what way the findings will turn out to be contingent on some fortuitously present characteristic of the subject—until the investigation is repeated on an adequate sample of persons. As excellent a way as it is to make discoveries, the study of an individual cannot be used to establish laws.

## The nomothetic approach

Most psychologists subscribe to the nomothetic approach: they carry out experiments on groups of subjects, and then attempt to generalise their findings to other non-observed populations. One obvious point in favour of this approach is that it seems to have worked rather well in practice, in the sense that much of value has been discovered by its use.

As Cronbach (1957) pointed out, most experimental psychologists simply ignored individual differences altogether. The position has changed only relatively little in the intervening years, as most experimental and cognitive psychologists still studiously avoid taking such differences into account. Why should this be the case?

Presumably, these psychologists believe individual differences are of only minor consequence in determining behaviour, and that behaviour depends mainly on the particular situation one is in at any given moment. However, the evidence clearly indicates that this is incorrect. Bowers (1973) compared the relative importance of individual differences and of the situation in determining behaviour in 11 different studies, using the percentage of the variance accounted for as the measure: the larger this percentage, the more important a factor is in influencing behaviour. On average, the situation accounted for 10.17% of the variance and the person (i.e. individual differences) accounted for 11.27%. In other words, individual differences and the situation are of approximately equal importance in determining behaviour, and the position adopted by experimental and cognitive psychologists is unwarranted.

It would obviously be of value to compare the idiographic and nomothetic approaches directly in terms of their ability to make accurate predictions. Research relevant to this issue was reviewed by Meehl (1954).

He considered 20 studies in which attempts were made to predict outcomes such as the recovery of psychiatric patients and criminals' relapse into crime using two different methods. The *clinical method* was based on interviews or case studies followed by subjective judgement, and resembled the idiographic approach; the *statistical method* was based on making predictions by comparing scores on standardised tests to population norms, and resembled the nomothetic approach.

The statistical or nomothetic approach proved more successful in approximately half of the studies, and the two methods were equally successful in the other studies. Although these findings suggest that the nomothetic approach is superior, subsequent research has indicated that a combination of the two methods can be better than either on its own.

## Conclusions

It is likely that many of those involved in the nomothetic–idiographic controversy have exaggerated the problems associated with reconciling the two approaches. It is entirely possible, for example, that there are general principles influencing people's behaviour, and that every individual's uniqueness can be understood as resulting from the impact of those general principles on their experiences.

A possible compromise position was proposed by H.J. Eysenck (1966). He argued that experimental or nomothetic psychologists should take account of some of the most important dimensions of individual differences in their research. More specifically, he proposed that people who are potential subjects for research should be assessed for their levels of intelligence, extraversion, and neuroticism, and then categorised as high, intermediate, or low on each dimension. In total, this would produce 27 different categories of subjects (e.g. high intelligence, intermediate extraversion, low neuroticism; intermediate intelligence, low extraversion, low neuroticism).

It would then be possible to carry out standard experiments using all 27 categories. In addition to observing the effects of the various independent variables on the dependent variable, it would also be possible to determine whether the impact of each independent variable was unusually great or small for any particular group of subjects. For example, being with other people might make people happier than being on their own, but this effect might be greater for those high in extraversion than for those low in extraversion

There are two major limitations of H.J. Eysenck's proposal. First, many psychologists do not agree that intelligence, extraversion, and neuroticism are the most important dimensions of individual differences. Second, there is the practical problem that experiments would need to be on a very large scale. Even relatively modest experiments would need to have several hundred subjects to ensure there were sufficient subjects in each of the 27 individual difference categories.

It should be noted that the relative value of the nomothetic and idiographic approaches depends greatly on the questions to which we want an answer. If, for example, we want to understand long-term memory, it is appropriate to employ the nomothetic approach and look at long-term memory in several people. On the other hand, if we want to predict a given individual's ability to show long-term memory of a set of learning materials, it is probably preferable to do an in-depth investigation of that person's memory system rather than relying on general theoretical views of memory functioning.

Another way of expressing the relative advantages and disadvantages of the two approaches was favoured by Malim et al. (1992). They argued that science has four main aims (description; understanding; prediction; and control); the idiographic approach is particularly useful in achieving the goals of description and understanding, whereas the nomothetic approach is better for attaining the goals of prediction and control.

# Consciousness

## Definition and functions

According to Boring (1929), consciousness can be defined as "direct awareness or immediate experience, the content of the mind as directly given to the experiencing person without the mediation of inference or any other intervening process" (p. 28). However, this definition is limited, because consciousness can refer to two somewhat different things: (1) sensory experience; and (2) a higher order self-consciousness, in which one is aware of being aware.

It follows from these definitions that consciousness plays a central role in most people's lives. We have conscious recollection of the past, conscious thoughts about the problems of everyday life, conscious anticipations of the future, and conscious awareness of the people and objects present in the visual environment. Through consciousness, we can reflect on our own position within our family, our friendship network, our workplace, or society in general.

One of the main difficulties with studying consciousness is that we cannot have direct knowledge of other people's conscious experience. Wittgenstein (1953) expressed the problems this raises by comparing each person's conscious experience with the contents of a box: "No-one can look into anyone else's box, and everyone says he knows what a beetle is only by looking at his beetle … it would be quite possible for everyone to have something different in his box … the box might even be empty" (paragraph 293).

In spite of these problems, there is fairly general agreement on some of the characteristics of conscious experience:

- it is private;
- it can combine information across different sensory modalities;
- it contains information about the results or products of thought processes rather than the processes themselves (e.g. if asked to name the capital of France, we think of the answer with no awareness of the processes involved in producing it);
- it is constantly changing like a river or a stream.

What are the functions of consciousness? Shallice (1982) and other psychologists have proposed that consciousness can be used in decision-making; it permits flexibility of behaviour; it can be used to control action; and it can be used to monitor behaviour. The result of a failure to monitor one's actions adequately is often absent-minded behaviour, in which a sequence of motor activities is run off in an automatic fashion. An example of such absent-minded behaviour was given by William James (1890): "Very absent-minded persons in going to their bedroom to dress for dinner have been known to take off one garment after another and finally to get

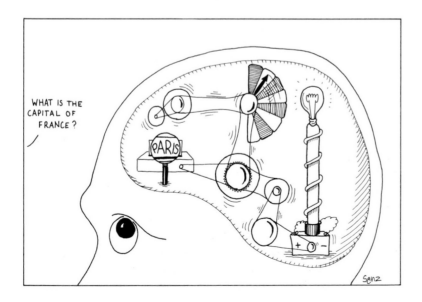

WHAT IS THE
CAPITAL OF
FRANCE ?

into bed, merely because that was the habitual issue of the first few movements when performed at a later hour".

## Dethroning of consciousness

We have the strong impression that our conscious experience provides us with reasonably accurate and complete information about the world and our place in it. An important issue is whether our impression of the power of consciousness is actually justified.

Sigmund Freud was one of the first psychologists to embark on the task of dethroning consciousness from its key position within psychology. He believed that much human behaviour is determined by the unconscious, and mental disorder can only be understood by probing beneath the conscious level into the seamy depths of the unconscious. However, powerful research evidence indicating that a substantial amount of information processing occurs below the level of consciousness has only been carried out within the past 20 years or so. There are at least four major strands of research to be considered:

- Introspection: Nisbett and Wilson (1977) studied the decision-making processes, and found that people often have very poor conscious awareness of the true reasons why they behaved in a particular way (see next section of this chapter).
- Cognitive neuropsychology: brain-damaged patients often behave appropriately in spite of having no conscious awareness of the knowledge underlying their behaviour. Claparede (1911) concealed a pin in his hand before shaking hands with a female patient suffering from amnesia (memory loss). The next day the patient was reluctant to shake hands with him, but could give no reason for her reluctance.
- Automatic processes: there is substantial evidence that prolonged practice at a task often leads to the development of automatic processes and a reduction in conscious awareness of how task behaviour is being produced (see Eysenck & Keane, 1990). For example, expert typists generally have little or no conscious awareness of where the letters are on a keyboard, despite having typed each letter thousands of times. The knowledge is "in the fingers", and the typists have to mimic the appropriate finger action in order to identify the locations of the letters.
- Priming effects: Tulving, Schacter, and Stark (1982) carried out an experiment in which a list of words was presented, followed by a word-fragment task asking subjects to think of a word fitting the fragments (e.g. ASSASSIN for the word fragment A—A—IN). Subjects were more successful at completing word fragments when the

appropriate word had been presented in the original word list; this is known as a priming effect. Significantly, the priming effect was found even for list words that subjects had no conscious experience of having seen before. In other words, the presentation of words on a list improved memory performance as assessed by the word-fragment task, even when there was no conscious recollection of the words having been presented.

One way of developing a greater understanding of consciousness is by studying different states of consciousness, or brain activity, such as hypnosis and the various stages of sleep. There is also evidence that some drugs can produce altered states of consciousness, but this is mostly anecdotal rather than properly scientific. For example, Albert Hoffman (1967) described his experiences after taking the hallucinogen lysergic acid diethylamide, better known as LSD: "My visual field wavered and everything appeared deformed as in a faulty mirror ... I was overcome by a fear that I was going out of my mind. The worst part of it being that I was clearly aware of my condition ... I thought I had died. My ego seemed suspended somewhere in space, from where I saw my dead body lying on the sofa". Those who have taken LSD commonly report such terrifying thoughts and images, and also often claim to have had important new insights. Close examination usually reveals such "insights" to be of no lasting value.

## Hypnosis

Hypnosis is a state that can be induced in many people as a result of being given repeated suggestions by a hypnotist to relax and fixate on some object (such as a swinging watch chain). The hypnotised individual appears to be in a relatively passive and sleep-like state, but recordings of brain-wave activity indicate the hypnotic state bears little physiological resemblance to sleep.

Hypnotised individuals exhibit a wide range of interesting behaviour patterns, many indicating they are in a highly suggestible state. Some people respond to suggestions from the hypnotist by hallucinating—they may imagine a dangerous animal is in the room, and respond with every appearance of fear. Hypnotised individuals also show relatively little sensitivity to pain; as a consequence, hypnosis has been used medically to assist dental patients and women in labour.

Other phenomena are age regression (in which events from childhood are relived); and post-hypnotic suggestion (the individual after hypnosis behaves in a way suggested during hypnosis). For example, the hypnotist may suggest the person will start to sneeze when the hypnotist looks at his watch; but if the individual does sneeze at the appropriate moment, he or she won't realise what has triggered this behaviour. Another alleged characteristic of the hypnotised state is its association with improved memory, leading police forces in several countries to use hypnosis to extract useful information from eyewitnesses to crimes and accidents.

The crucial question about hypnosis is whether or not it represents a special, altered state of consciousness. The most prominent advocate of the view that it does so is Ernest Hilgard (1986), who proposed a *neo-dissociation theory*. Hypnotic phenomena occur because there is a dissociation (separating off) of one part of the body's system from the rest by means of *amnesic barriers*. For example, hypnotised individuals exposed to painful stimuli typically exhibit the normal physiological responses associated with pain, even though they deny experiencing much pain. This suggests that the part of the brain registering conscious awareness of pain is separated off from those parts registering basic physiological responses.

Although hypnosis appears superficially to involve a very strange and special state of consciousness, there are reasons for arguing that it is not actually very different from naturally occurring states. First, some of the phenomena found in hypnotised individuals are rather suspect. The enhanced memory claimed for hypnosis is, for example, an illusion—hypnotised people are simply less cautious in their reporting of memories. As a consequence, genuine memories are sometimes recalled, but so are numerous inaccurate memories. The fallibility of memories reported under hypnosis is illustrated by the fact that hypnotised individuals will confidently claim to "remember" events from the future!

Second, and most important, nearly all the phenomena associated with hypnosis have also been observed in non-hypnotised individuals. People who are highly motivated and given the appropriate expectations can mimic most of the behaviour of hypnotised individuals. Indeed, Orne found that a well-trained hypnotist couldn't distinguish between hypnotised individuals and others who had been given practice in behaving as if they were hypnotised.

Third, it is generally accepted that hypnotised individuals are highly suggestible. This implies that many phenomena associated with hypnosis can be explained simply as attempts to conform to the wishes of the hypnotist, rather than by recourse to notions of an altered state of consciousness.

## Sleep and dreaming

Our understanding of what happens in the brain during sleep has been greatly enhanced by the use of psychophysiological measures; the electro-

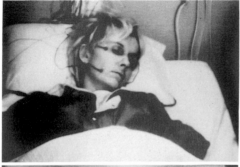

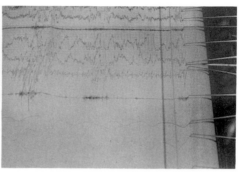

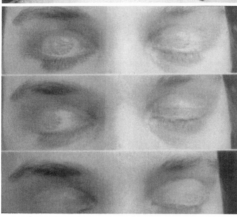

Top left: Infra-red picture of a sleeper being monitored at a sleep research laboratory (Photo courtesy Philippe Plailly/ Science Photo Library). Top right: Sominography equipment used to monitor a variety of physiological measurements including EEG and muscle movements around the eye (Photo courtesy Peter Menzel/ Science Photo Library). Bottom left: Eye movement during REM sleep, the deepest of the five stages of sleep. During this stage, the muscles of the eyes are in constant motion behind the closed eyelids. People woken abruptly during REM sleep often report that they were dreaming at the time (photo courtesty Alan Hobson/Science Photo Library.)

encephalograph or EEG has been of particular value. In essence, scalp electrodes are used to obtain a continuous measure of brain-wave activity, recorded as a trace on a long sheet of paper revolving on a drum. Other psychophysiological measures include eye-movement data from an elec-tro-oculogram or EOG; and muscle movements from an electromyogram or EMG.

Evidence primarily from the EEG has revealed the existence of five different stages of sleep:

Stage 1: the EEG is irregular, there is slow eye rolling, and the heart rate slows. During this rather shallow period of sleep, the sleeper can readily be woken up.

Stage 2: sleep spindles appear in the EEG record, and there is little activity in the EOG.

Stage 3: the EOG and EMG resemble stage 2, but there are long slow delta waves in the EEG instead of sleep spindles. This is a deeper sleep than is found in the first two stages.

Stage 4: there is a predominance of the long slow delta waves present in smaller quantities in the previous stage, and relatively little activity in the EOG or the EMG.

Stage 5: rapid eye movement or REM sleep, characterised by rapid eye movements and a very low level of EMG activity, while the EEG record resembles that of stage 1. REM sleep has sometimes been called paradoxical sleep, because it is more difficult to awaken someone from REM sleep than from any of the other stages, even though the EEG indicates the brain is very active.

After the sleeper has worked through the first four stages of progressively deeper sleep, he or she reverses the process: stage 4 is followed by stage 3 and then by stage 2. However, stage 2 is followed by REM sleep (stage 5). After REM sleep, the sleeper starts another sleep cycle, working his or her way through stages 2, 3, and 4, followed by stage 3, then stage 2, and then REM sleep again. A complete sleep cycle (known as an ultradian cycle) lasts for approximately 90 minutes, and the average sleeper will complete about five ultradian cycles during a normal night's sleep. The proportion of the cycle devoted to REM sleep tends to increase progressively from one cycle to the next.

From the psychologist's point of view, the most interesting stage is REM sleep. There is strong evidence that dreaming normally occurs during this stage: if people are awoken from REM sleep, more than three-quarters of the time they report having just been dreaming; in contrast, the figure is only approximately 15% if they are awoken from other stages of sleep. As Gross (1987) pointed out, REM sleep has sometimes been referred to as the "third state of existence", because it differs considerably from both the waking state and the normal sleeping state.

The dream state is very distinctive, and it is natural to enquire into the reasons why we dream. Most people report that their dreams are often incoherent and sometimes even bizarre, and there are various theories as to why dreams have this incoherent quality. Probably the most obvious reason is that the processes which control and direct our conscious thought during the waking day are inactive while we are asleep.

However, a more physiologically based activation-synthesis theory was proposed by Hobson and McCarley (1977): the physiological mechanisms responsible for dreaming produce high levels of activation in several different parts of the brain, including those involved in perception, action, and emotional reactions. The dreamer attempts to synthesise (combine) information from these different areas of activity, but the result is often rather incoherent.

Another theory is based on the fact that many (or most) dreams refer to events experienced by the dreamer during the previous day, and one of the main functions of dreaming is probably to try to make sense of our day-by-day experiences—but these attempts are often unsuccessful and result in incoherent dreams.

The best-known theory was proposed by Sigmund Freud, who claimed that all dreams represent *wish fulfilment*, primarily of repressed desires (e.g. sexual). However, because of the unacceptability of these wish fulfilments, the actual dream and its meaning (the *latent content*) have generally been distorted into a more acceptable form (the *manifest content*) by the time the dreamer is consciously aware of his or her dream. Psychoanalysis (see Chapter 2) can be used to uncover the latent content—according to Freud, dream analysis provides a *via regia* (royal road) to an understanding of the unconscious mind.

There are various problems with Freud's theory. Some dreams (nightmares) are very frightening, and it is often difficult to regard them as wish fulfilling even in a distorted fashion. More importantly, the latent content of a dream as identified through psychoanalysis generally appears rather arbitrary and open to question. Although some dreams undoubtedly represent wish fulfilment (and not always in a distorted form!), it is unlikely that all dreams can reasonably be regarded as wish fulfilling.

## Introspection

Views about the usefulness of introspection (the examination of one's own thoughts) have varied enormously over the centuries. At one extreme, Aristotle argued that introspection was the only way of studying thinking; at the other, Sir Francis Galton claimed the position of consciousness "appears to be that of a helpless spectator of but a minute fraction of automatic brain work". As we have seen, much information processing goes on below the level of conscious awareness, and this necessarily limits the usefulness of introspection.

Most psychologists nowadays probably accept that introspection is often (but not always) a useful technique, but there are a number of dissident voices. Nisbett and Wilson (1977) argued forcefully that introspection is practically worthless.

One of the experiments they cited as support for their position involved presenting a horizontal array of essentially identical pairs of stockings. Subjects had to decide which pair was the best, and then indicate why they had chosen that particular pair. They typically justified their choices by claiming the chosen pair was slightly superior in colour or texture to other pairs. In fact, this introspective evidence was well wide of the mark: most subjects chose the right-most pair, and thus their choices were actually influenced by relative spatial position. But even when they were specifi-

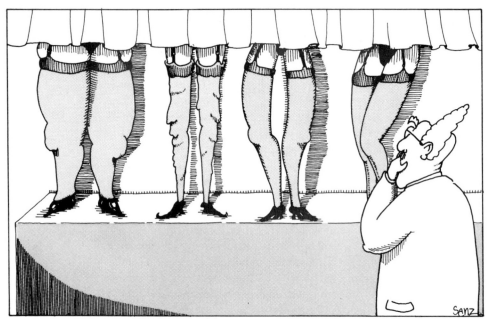

ON REFLECTION, DR. TOPTURF WONDERED IF POSITIONING *WAS* THE ONLY INFLUENTIAL FACTOR.

cally asked whether the position of the selected pair of stockings in the array might have affected their choice, they vehemently denied it.

Of course, people can sometimes provide an accurate account of their own mental processes, which might suggest that introspective evidence can be valuable. However, Nisbett and Wilson argued that this view is mistaken. They pointed out that an individual's introspections about why he or she is behaving in a particular way are generally no more accurate than the guesses about the determinants of that behaviour made by other people who observe it. This suggests that introspection fails to give "magical access" to important information about our own thought processes.

It is certainly true that introspective evidence can be remarkably uninformative, and even misleading. A striking example is the phenomenon of *blind sight*, investigated in detail by Weiskrantz (1986). His patient DB had an operation which left him with an area of subjective blindness in his visual field, within which he claimed to be able to see nothing. In spite of this absence of introspective evidence, DB could decide whether a light was present or absent in the "blind" part of his visual field. He could also distinguish between moving and stationary objects, and decide whether a stimulus was in the visual field. In all these cases, DB felt he was simply guessing, and was very surprised to discover the accuracy of his guesses. It is this discrepancy between introspective evidence about visual perception and the objective evidence of accurate guessing which defines the phenomenon of "blind sight".

If Nisbett and Wilson are right, introspection cannot be used as a method within a scientific approach to psychology. However, there are strong doubts as to whether they are more than partially correct. A more balanced view of introspection was provided by Ericsson and Simon (1980), who argued that the validity of introspective evidence depends on various factors:

- introspection obtained during the performance of a task is more likely to be valid than introspection obtained retrospectively, after a task is finished;
- introspection is more valuable when it refers to the object of an individual's attention or thought than when it involves interpretive processes (e.g. why the individual has done something);
- introspection is valid only when concerned with information on which the individual is focusing.

It is of interest to relate Ericcson and Simon's arguments to the experimental studies used by Nisbett and Wilson to illustrate the invalidity of introspection. In nearly all those studies (e.g. the stocking experiment), the introspective evidence was obtained retrospectively, involved interpretations of behaviour, and concerned information that had not been the focus of attention. In other words, Nisbett and Wilson actually demonstrated only that there are some circumstances in which introspection is valueless.

# Summary

- Psychology is closely related to other sciences, and *reductionists* propose that human behaviour can ultimately be explained by more basic scientific disciplines such as physiology and biochemistry.
- The term reductionism also refers to attempts to account for complex phenomena in terms of simple processes.
- Reductionism in both senses has been generally unsuccessful so far, although there are probably cases in which a reductionist explanation is appropriate.
- There has been fierce controversy over *determinism versus free will*: determinists argue that all human behaviour could potentially be explained as resulting from some definite cause or causes, and we are thus under the control of our heredity and environment; believers in free will argue that we are free to make whatever decisions we want in life.
- The seemingly huge gulf between the two points of view may be more apparent than real—it is possible that the processes involved in free will could be incorporated into a deterministic theory.
- The issue of the relative importance of *nature and nurture* has been the source of much controversy, but most psychologists are coming to adopt a sensible compromise which accepts that heredity and environment both contribute to individual differences in behaviour.
- A more systematic analysis of the ways in which heredity and environment interact and combine to determine behaviour is now required.
- According to the *idiographic* approach every individual is unique, and so psychology should be based on a detailed analysis of individuals rather than of groups.
- In contrast, *nomothetic* psychologists (who are in a majority) argue psychology is a science, and as such should be concerned primarily with general laws.
- It is possible to accommodate individual uniqueness within the nomothetic approach, so idiographic and nomothetic approaches can be reconciled.
- Conscious experience is typically private, constantly changing, combines information across modalities, and contains information about the results of thought processes rather than the processes themselves.
- Most people feel their conscious thoughts provide reasonably accurate information about the outside world and their place in it; but there appear to be numerous exceptions to the accuracy of this belief—in particular, there is increasing evidence that much information processing goes on below the level of conscious awareness.

- Attempts have been made to understand consciousness more thoroughly by studying phenomena such as *hypnosis* and *sleep*.
- It remains unclear whether or not hypnosis represents an altered state of consciousness, but there is good evidence for the existence of various different stages of sleep.
- Introspection relies on conscious awareness and is sometimes useful, especially when individuals are reporting the thoughts they are having at that moment.
- Introspection is generally less useful when individuals provide retrospective reports, and are asked to interpret or explain their experience.

"AND SO WE CONCLUDE... THAT IF WE LOOK DEEP WITHIN OURSELVES, WE FIND THAT INTROSPECTION IS WORTHLESS..."

# 4 Motivation and emotion

**P**hilosophers used to argue that the mind and behaviour could only be understood by considering cognition, conation (motivation), and affect (emotion). The knowledge we possess is determined by the workings of the cognitive system, the goals towards which we strive are determined by the motivational system, and the feelings that we experience are determined by the emotional system. It thus follows that motivation and emotion are of special significance in human psychology.

This chapter is concerned with the concepts of motivation and emotion, which are complex in various ways. Motivational and emotional states are both caused by a mixture of internal and external factors: for example, someone may feel hungry because he or she has not eaten for several hours (internal factor) or because tempting food is visible (external factor).

Motivation and emotion are complex concepts in another way. Many (or most) of our emotions and motives depend on the physiological, cognitive, and behavioural systems combining or interacting in complex ways with each other. Although nearly everyone agrees that all three systems need to be considered, there has been much controversy because theorists differ among themselves as to which of these systems is most important.

We have seen that motivation and emotion resemble each other in various ways. Sometimes they are very closely related. For example, if a dog is administered an electric shock in a box and is then placed back in the box, it will act in an anxious emotional fashion. In addition, however, it will be motivated to escape from the box in order to reduce its level of anxiety. In other words, anxiety can function as an emotion and also as a motive, and the same may be true of some other emotions.

## Motivation

Psychologists have differed among themselves in their definitions of motivation, but there is reasonable agreement that it is highly relevant to the following:

- *direction of behaviour*: the goal or goals being pursued;
- *intensity of behaviour*: the amount of effort, concentration, and so on, invested in behaviour;
- *persistence of behaviour*: the extent to which a goal is pursued until it is reached.

A definition incorporating these ingredients was proposed by Taylor et al. (1982): "Motivation ... is generally conceived of by psychologists in terms of a process, or a series of processes, which somehow starts, steers, sustains and finally stops a goal-directed sequence of behaviour" (p. 160).

This view of motivation can be illustrated in terms of an example. If someone is very hungry, we would expect their behaviour to be directed towards the goals of finding and eating food, we would expect them to put in a considerable amount of effort, and we would expect them to continue looking for food until they discovered some.

The notion that motivated behaviour is behaviour directed towards a particular goal carries with it some problems for psychologists. First, there is the problem of deciding whether or not a particular pattern of behaviour is actually goal-directed. Instead of simply claiming that all behaviour is goal-directed and so motivated, it is probably more accurate to assume that behaviour can vary in the extent to which it is goal-directed or motivated. This implies there will be cases in which it is difficult to be sure whether behaviour is sufficiently goal-directed to qualify as motivated.

Second, there has been considerable disagreement as to how much of human behaviour is goal-directed or motivated. One of those who argued strongly that all behaviour is motivated was McDougall (1912). According to him there are numerous fundamental motives, which he called *instincts* or *propensities*, including food-seeking, sex, curiosity, fear, parental protectiveness, disgust, anger, laughter, self-assertiveness, gregariousness, acquisitiveness, rest, migration, appeal for assistance, comfort, submissiveness, and constructiveness.

With such a long and varied list, McDougall could account for all behaviour by attributing it to the attempt to satisfy one or other of these instincts. However, most psychologists have doubted whether it makes much sense to identify so many instincts—for example, the idea that migration, constructiveness, or submissiveness are fundamental motives seems improbable. Another problem is that there is a great danger of circular argument—for example, to argue that someone is being self-assertive because of their self-assertiveness instinct does not really explain their behaviour! Instead of desperately trying to explain all behaviour by one or other instinct, it may

WITH MOUNTING APPREHENSION, TREVOR BEGAN TO SUSPECT THAT THE REMOTE CONTROL HAD ONCE MORE BEEN PLACED OUT OF ARM'S REACH.

well be preferable to assume that at least some human behaviour (such as slumping in front of a television set) is essentially unmotivated.

## Categorising motives

Even if McDougall's long list of instincts must be rejected, several different motives clearly need to be identified. Various attempts have been made to classify these motives for theoretical purposes: one system is based on distinguishing between motives that are *internally aroused*, and those that are *externally aroused*. The motives for food, drink, sleep, and elimination all depend importantly on internal factors, whereas motives such as a desire to avoid extreme temperatures or to withdraw from painful stimulation are triggered off by external stimuli.

However, it would be unwise to draw too sharp a distinction, as most motives depend on a mixture of internal and external factors. For example, although the goal of eating often depends importantly on internal physiological conditions, it is also affected by external stimuli such as the sight of appetising food. Another clear example is sexual motivation, which is certainly affected by sex hormones in the bloodstream, but also influenced by external factors such as the presence and availability of an attractive partner.

A related way of categorising motives is into *cyclic* and *non-cyclic*. Cyclic motives are those where the motivational force increases and decreases in a more or less regular and predictable way over time. Thus, for example, the needs to sleep and to eat clearly constitute cyclic motives, whereas the motive to avoid painful stimulation does not. In general terms, cyclic motives tend to be internally aroused, whereas non-cyclic motives are externally aroused.

One of the most useful ways of classifying motives is into *primary* or *basic* and *secondary* or *acquired*. Primary drives or motives are those which appear without the necessity for learning, and which are found in virtually every member of a species. They include the need for food, the need for drink, and the need for elimination. According to Taylor et al. (1982), curiosity and the need to form atttachments to others should also be regarded as primary motives. Secondary drives or motives are learned, and it is usually assumed that their existence owes much to primary drives. For example, many people regard the acquisition of money as an important goal in its own right, but the initial importance of money is simply as a way of being able to satisfy primary motives, such as those for food and drink.

Another approach to categorisation within motivation theory is to construct a *hierarchy of motives*. As we saw in Chapter 2, the clinical psychologist Abraham Maslow (1968) suggested a hierarchy of basic human needs. The needs for food, drink, warmth, and shelter are at the bottom, and the need for self-actualisation is at the top. In between are several other needs such as those for protection against dangers, for affection, for self-respect, and cognitive needs (e.g. curiosity) and aesthetic needs.

## Theories of motivation

*Homeostatic drive theory* was one of the early major theories of motivation. It was based on the notion of *homeostasis*, which was used by Cannon (1929) to refer to the processes by which we maintain a reasonably constant internal environment. For example, body temperature in healthy individuals varies only slightly whether they are in a cold or a hot climate. If body temperature increases in a hot climate, then sweating occurs to correct the imbalance and return body temperature to its normal level.

The basic idea in homeostatic drive theory is that many different kinds of internal imbalance produce homeostatic drives, which prompt the behaviour needed to correct the imbalance and thus restore equilibrium or homeostasis. For example, hunger has various physiological effects

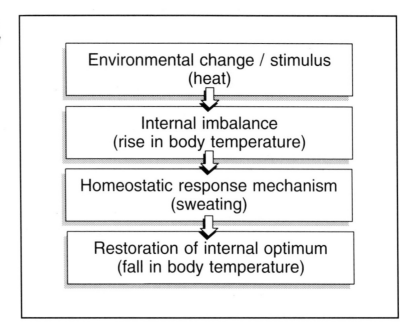

which lead us to search for food, because eating reduces the internal discomfort caused by hunger.

There was important research in the 1950s and 1960s which appeared to identify the hypothalamus as that part of the brain crucially involved in hunger. In essence, it appeared that activation of the lateral hypothalamus causes animals to start eating, whereas activation of the ventro-medial nucleus of the hypothalamus produces a cessation of eating. As Gross (1992) pointed out, this simple view of hunger is not accurate. The hypothalamus is not itself the main brain structure involved in hunger; rather, it acts as a transmitting station to other parts of the brain which have a more vital role in hunger drive.

Hull (1943) expanded homeostatic drive theory in various ways. He drew a distinction between *needs*, which are essentially physiological in nature, and *drives*, which are less physiological and more psychological. Drives derive from needs such as those for food, water, sex, and so on. Hull's approach was called *drive-reduction theory* because it was assumed that behaviour is motivated by the attempt to reduce one or more drives. Drive reduction is reinforcing or rewarding, so that animals learn to behave in ways that will lead to drive reduction. For example, if a young child learns that eating biscuits from a jar in the kitchen reduces hunger drive, then he or she will show an increased tendency to return to the biscuit jar in the future when hungry.

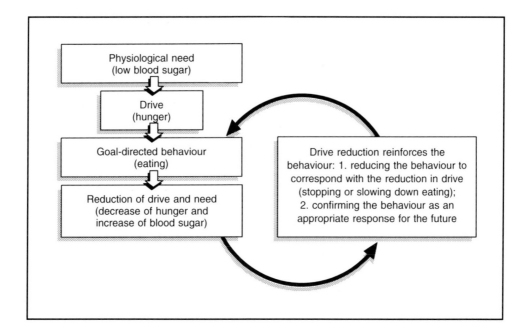

A central assumption in Hull's drive-reduction theory was the notion that the behaviour an organism will display in a given situation is determined by drive or motivation, and by what it has learned (habits). This led to the equation that the tendency to respond = drive × habit. Subsequently, Hull added further assumptions about the role of incentives and other factors. However, he still maintained that behaviour depends mainly on a combination of motivation (drive) and learning (habit).

Drive reduction theory

The general approach represented by homeostatic drive theory and drive-reduction theory has fallen into disfavour in recent years. Why should this be the case?

First, there are numerous exceptions to the notion that all behaviour is directed towards drive reduction. Much human behaviour is based on curiosity, and it is difficult to regard curiosity as involving the reduction of either a drive or a need. It has been found that rats who receive electrical stimulation of a particular part of their brain for pressing a lever will do so thousands of times an hour for several hours (Olds & Milner, 1954). Again, no physiological need is reduced by this behaviour.

Second, the theoretical approach was based very largely on experiments with other species. It is possible (if unlikely) that rats, dogs, and other species are largely motivated to reduce physiological needs and drives, but it is much less likely that this is true of humans. For example, the humanistic psychologists argued that humans are motivated by cognitive needs (such as curiosity), aesthetic or artistic needs, and the need for self-actualisation, as well as by the basic needs for food, water, and so on. Whether one agrees with the humanistic approach or not, it is probable that the forces which motivate humans are much more numerous than was envisaged in drive-reduction theory.

Third, there is very little recognition in drive-reduction theory that cognitive factors play an important role in human motivation. As we will see later in this chapter, some theorists (e.g. Locke, 1968) have argued that motivation depends in large measure on the goals which we have set ourselves—for example, someone who is firmly committed to obtaining a B grade in A-level psychology is likely to be more motivated and will work harder than someone who is only concerned about passing. This aspect of motivation was ignored by Cannon and Hull.

Drive-reduction theorists focused mainly on the role of physiological factors in motivation. In contrast, Deci (1971; 1975) proposed a *theory of intrinsic motivation* bearing some resemblance to the humanistic approach. According to his theory, performance on a task is *intrinsically motivated* when the task activity provides the only apparent source of reward, possibly in the form of enhanced feelings of competence and self-determination. Intrinsic motivation is closely related to some of Maslow's higher-level needs (such as the need for self-esteem).

In contrast, performance on a task is *extrinsically motivated* when the motivation is produced by external rewards and incentives (such as money). Skinner is an example of a psychologist who emphasised the importance of extrinsic motivation. For example, he discovered that rats could be motivated to press a lever hundreds of times an hour provided that they were occasionally given reinforcement or reward in the form of a food pellet.

It is natural to assume that extrinsic and intrinsic motivation combine together to determine an individual's total level of motivation. However, Deci (1975) challenged this assumption, arguing that increasing extrinsic motivation often reduces intrinsic motivation. According to his theory, extrinsic rewards or incentives make people feel their behaviour is controlled by external forces, and this then reduces their feelings of self-determination, and undermines their intrinsic motivation. An example of this may be found in professional sportspeople, who often seem to enjoy their chosen sport less when they are paid for doing it well.

Experimental evidence to support this theory was obtained by Deci (1971). Subjects who had previously received payment (extrinsic rewards) for solving complicated block-arrangement problems were less inclined to spend their leisure time working on further problems than were those who had never been financially rewarded. In other words, extrinsic rewards served to reduce intrinsic motivation.

There has been an increased tendency in recent years to recognise that cognitive factors are relevant to motivation. Locke (1968) proposed a very influential cognitive theory of motivation. According to his *goal theory*, the key ingredient in motivation is the goal, defined as "what the individual is consciously trying to do" (p. 159). The goal that someone has set himself or herself can be assessed by direct questioning.

How does goal setting relate to performance? According to Locke (1968), there is a straightforward relationship between goal difficulty and performance: "the harder the goal the higher the level of performance" (p. 162). This was predicted because people exert more effort and utilise more resources when difficult goals are set.

Goal theory has been especially influential in *work psychology*. For example, Latham and Yukl (1975) divided workers whose job was cutting and transporting wood into three categories: groups simply instructed to "do your best" but not required to set a goal (do-your-best groups); groups assigned a specific hard goal in terms of hundreds of cubic feet of wood per week (assigned groups); and groups in which everyone participated in setting a specific hard production goal (participative groups). The average goal in the participative groups was about 8% higher than in the assigned groups.

According to Locke's theory, we would expect the participative groups to perform best, because they set the hardest goals; the assigned groups to come next; and the do-your-best groups to do worst, because they did not set themselves difficult goals. The findings were as predicted: The do-your-best groups averaged 46 cubic feet of wood an hour, the assigned groups averaged 53 cubic feet, and the participative groups averaged 56 cubic feet.

The evidence on goal theory was reviewed by Locke, Shaw, Saari, and Latham (1981). They concluded that goal setting improved performance in approximately 90% of the studies, but was especially likely to do so under the following conditions:

- *goal commitment*: individuals accept the goal which has been set;
- *feedback*: information about progress towards goals is provided;
- *rewards*: goal attainment is rewarded;
- *ability*: individuals have sufficient ability to attain the goal;
- *support*: management provides encouragement.

How useful is goal theory? On the positive side, it has established itself as one of the leading theories of motivation in the workplace. It has also been fairly consistently supported by the experimental evidence (Locke et al., 1981). Another advantage is that it sheds some light on individual differences in motivation: highly motivated workers set higher goals and are more committed to them than are poorly motivated workers.

On the negative side, it provides a somewhat limited approach to motivation. It is often not clear exactly why some individuals set higher goals than others. In addition, major motivating forces such as hunger and thirst are not considered.

In sum, we have considered a few of the many theories of motivation that have been proposed over the years. The theories differ substantially—in general terms, more recent theories of motivation emphasise cognitive factors and higher-level needs, whereas earlier theories emphasise physiological factors and lower-level needs.

It is probable that an adequate theory of motivation (if it is ever possible to construct one) will combine aspects of these various theories in a broader framework. Maslow included numerous needs in his hierarchy of needs, ranging from the basic (food, water) to the high-level needs (such as self-actualisation), and so his theory was more comprehensive than the ones we have considered in this section. Unfortunately, Maslow's theory possesses great weaknesses and cannot be regarded as scientifically based (see Chapter 2). The search for an adequate theory of motivation continues.

## The value of the motivational concept

Is the concept of motivation of continuing usefulness? The fact that most (or all) behaviour is motivated may mean the concept of motivation is almost useless, because a concept which is used to explain everything is in danger of explaining nothing.

As Taylor et al. (1982, p. 190) pointed out:

> it has been argued that motivation is not a topic in its own right at all, precisely because its applicability is total ... it may be more profitable for psychologists interested in motivational phenomena to ask not "why" such behaviour occurs but rather "how" it occurs—how sequences of goal-directed behaviour develop, how they are sustained and how they come to be terminated. When this is done, the motivational concepts on which psychologists have traditionally relied may be of comparatively little use in providing satisfactory explanations of goal-directed behaviour.

It is certainly true that motivation in the sense of goal-directed behaviour is a very broad topic. People can strive for an enormously large number of diverse goals: the goal can be very long-term (such as achieving a successful career) or very short-term (such as watching a film); it can be closely related to basic physiological processes (eating when hungry, for example) or it can be far removed from such processes (painting a picture). In view of such considerations, it is possible that at some stage the concept of motivation will be consigned to the dustbin of history.

# Emotion

The study of *emotion* is of great importance to psychologists, but it has proved rather difficult to provide an adequate definition of what we mean by "emotion". According to Drever (1964), emotion "is a complex state of the organism, involving bodily changes of a widespread character—in breathing, pulse, gland secretion, etc.—and, on the mental side, a state of excitement or perturbation, marked by a strong feeling, and usually an impulse towards a definite form of behaviour" (p. 82).

## The components of emotion

Emotions can be contrasted with moods, which are generally longer-lasting and less intense than emotions. Drever's definition of emotion makes it clear there are various different aspects or components to emotional states, and we may perhaps go beyond Drever to identify the components of emotion:

- *cognitive* or *thinking*: emotions are typically directed towards objects (e.g. we are in an anxious emotional state because the situation is dangerous, and we know the situation is dangerous rather than innocuous as a result of cognitive activity);
- *physiological*: there are typically a number of bodily changes involved in emotion; many of these (such as increased heart rate, increased blood pressure, increased respiration rate, sweating) occur because of arousal in the sympathetic division of the autonomic nervous system;
- *experiential*: the feelings experienced, which obviously cannot be assessed with species other than man;
- *expressive*: facial expression and other aspects of non-verbal behaviour such as bodily posture;
- *behavioural*: the pattern of behaviour (fight or flight) produced by an emotional state.

We might assume that all five components of the emotional response would generally be in *concordance* (agreement) with each other. For example, if someone is placed in a dangerous situation, one would expect substantial activity in the physiological component, conscious feelings of anxiety (e.g. on self-report questionnaires), an anxious facial expression, and appropriate behavioural signs (such as flight or impaired performance). In fact, a lack of concordance is typically found. For example, Craske and Craig (1984) considered the physiological, experiential, and behavioural components of anxiety in a study of competent pianists performing in public. They discovered that although measures belonging to the same component tended to correlate significantly with each other, measures from different components showed very little concordance or agreement.

What are the implications of a lack of concordance of the physiological, experiential, expressive, and behavioural components for the study of emotion? First, a lack of concordance means an adequate theory of emotion would have to be rather complex—it would need to explain why an individual can appear to be very anxious, angry, or whatever when one component of emotion is considered, but not when a different component is assessed.

Second, there are implications for experimental studies of emotion. If the different components were in agreement with each other, it would only be necessary to measure one component to assess the subject's emotional state. In fact, because each component tells a different story, it is important to measure all of them.

## Theories of emotion

The first systematic theory of emotion was put forward independently in America by William James and in Denmark by Lange; for obvious reasons, it later came to be known as the *James-Lange theory*. According to the theory, there are three stages in emotion:

1. an emotional stimulus is presented;
2. this produces bodily changes (such as arousal in the autonomic nervous system);
3. feedback from the bodily changes leads to the experience of emotion.

These three stages can be seen in the following example taken from James (1890): "I see a bear, I run away, I feel afraid". Stage 1 is seeing the bear, running away is stage 2, and feeling afraid is stage 3. Of course, most of us do not encounter many bears in our everyday lives. However, anyone who has nearly been knocked down by a car would probably agree that they jumped out of the way before feeling emotionally upset—as predicted by the James-Lange theory.

As Gross (1987) pointed out, there is some support for the theory in a rather unusual study carried out by Laird (1974). Students watched cartoons while contorting their facial expressions so that they were smiling, frowning, or whatever. The key finding was that the facial expression had an impact on the students' emotional state: for example, smiling increased happiness and frowing increased anger. These findings suggest that bodily changes can influence emotional experience as predicted by the James-Lange theory.

In spite of the successes of the theory, it is no longer regarded as adequate. Some of the major criticisms that the theory has attracted include the following: first, we often experience emotion before the bodily changes have occurred, rather than afterwards as the theory predicts. In other words, emotions can be triggered directly by an emotional stimulus rather than indirectly via bodily changes.

Second, it is assumed there is a distinctive pattern of bodily changes associated with each and every emotional state. There are several obvious examples of this—for example, smiling is associated with happiness, crying with unhappiness, and running away with anxiety. However, many different emotional states seem to be associated with a broadly similar state of arousal of the autonomic system, suggesting that the rich variety of emotional experience cannot depend solely on bodily changes.

Third, the theory states that an emotional stimulus produces a series of bodily changes. However, remarkably little is said about how this happens. It was left for contemporary theories (discussed shortly) to consider the ways in which the interpretation of a situation produces physiological and other effects.

The *Cannon-Bard theory* was proposed (e.g. Cannon, 1929) as an alternative to the James-Lange theory. According to the Cannon-Bard theory, when someone is placed in an emotional situation, a part of the brain known as the thalamus is activated. This is followed by two independent effects: (1) the appropriate emotional state is experienced; and (2) another part of the brain (the hypothalamus) is activated, and this produces physiological changes (such as arousal in the sympathetic division of the autonomic nervous system).

This theory has no problem with the fact that our conscious experience of emotion sometimes precedes the relevant bodily changes, because our emotional experience is more or less independent of those changes. However, it does suffer from some difficulties.

First, it seems unlikely that the bodily changes involved in emotion have no effect on our emotional experience. Paraplegics and quadriplegics, whose spinal cord injuries are so severe that they have little or no experience of physiological arousal, typically experience less intense emotions than other people. One reported: "Sometimes I act angry when I see some injustice. I yell and cuss and raise hell ... but it just doesn't have the heat to it that it used to. It's a kind of mental anger" (discussed in Eysenck & Eysenck, 1989). If perception of the bodily changes in emotion does not influence our emotional experience, why do some paraplegics and quadriplegics show reduced emotionality?

Second, it is not clear how perception of an emotional situation produces activation of the thalamus. For example, how does the cognitive system decide that a given situation is threatening or innocuous?

## Contemporary perspectives

The modern era in emotion research started with Schachter and Singer's (1962) very influential *cognitive labelling theory*. It owes much of its impact to the fact that it was one of the first theories of emotion to emphasise cognitive factors. In essence, they argued there are two factors, both of which are essential for emotion to be experienced: (1) high physiological arousal; and (2) an emotional interpretation (or label) of that arousal.

According to Schachter and Singer (1962), an emotional state will not be experienced if either of the two crucial factors is absent. An early study by Maranon (1924) is consistent with this prediction. Subjects were injected with adrenaline, a drug whose effects mimic almost perfectly a naturally occurring state of physiological arousal. When they were asked to say how they felt, 71% simply reported their physical symptoms with no emotional overtones. Most of the remaining subjects reported "as-if" or "cold" emotions. Why did practically none of the subjects report true emotions? Presumably they interpreted (or labelled) their state of arousal as having been produced by the drug, and so failed to attach an emotional label to it.

Schachter and Singer (1962) carried out an expanded version of Maranon's study. All the subjects were told the experiment was designed to test the effects of the vitamin compound Suproxin on vision. In fact, they were injected with either adrenaline or a saline solution having no effect on arousal. Some of those given adrenaline were correctly informed about the effects of the drug, whereas others were misinformed or uninformed (being told simply that the injection was mild and would have no side-effects). All the subjects given saline were told the drug would have no side-effects. Following the injection, the subjects were put in a situation designed to produce either euphoria or anger.

Which groups were the most emotional? Theoretically, it should have been those groups who received the adrenaline (and so were highly aroused) and who would not interpret the arousal as having been produced by the drug: that is, the misinformed and uninformed groups. The findings broadly supported these theoretical predictions, but many of the effects were rather small.

One of the problems with the Schachter and Singer study was that those subjects given saline may have become physiologically aroused as a result of being put in a euphoria- or anger-provoking situation. Schachter and Wheeler (1962) argued that the way to prevent people becoming aroused was to give them a drug that actually reduces arousal. The drug they chose for this purpose was the depressant chlorpromazine. Subjects were injected with chlorpromazine, adrenaline, or an ineffective placebo, and told that the drug had no side-effects. They then watched a slapstick film called "The Good Humour Man". As predicted, those injected with adrenaline (and thus aroused) found the film the funniest, whereas those injected with chlorpromazine (and thus de-aroused) found it least funny.

In spite of the impact it has had, cognitive labelling theory suffers from various limitations:

1. There is increasing evidence that does not support the theory. For example, Marshall and Zimbardo (1979) found that large doses of adrenaline actually reduced subjects' happiness in the euphoria condition. They argued that a high level of unexplained arousal is generally regarded as unpleasant, because high arousal is often associated with anxiety and stress.

2. The situation used by Schachter and Singer is very artificial. In our everyday lives, we rarely experience high levels of arousal that are difficult to interpret.

3. Schachter and Singer claimed that the same state of physiological arousal is associated with many different emotions. This is an over-simplification. Funkenstein (1955) found some support for the notion that anxiety is associated with the production of adrenaline, whereas noradrenaline release is associated with anger or aggression. Some emotional states (such as depression or grief) seem to be associated with rather low levels of arousal.

4. The cognitive labelling or interpretation of physiological arousal is of central importance in the Schachter-Singer theory. However, they had surprisingly little to say about the processes involved in labelling. Consider, for example, the arousal caused by being woken up in the middle of the night by a noise outside: why do

some people label this arousal "anxiety" whereas others do not? Presumably the way in which arousal is labelled in this situation depends on whether the situation is interpreted as a burglar trying to break in or as a cat knocking over milk bottles, but the theory does not really tell us what is happening.

In the Schachter-Singer theory, cognitive processes (i.e. cognitive labelling) happen after the physiological changes. However, many contemporary theorists argue that cognitive processes play a major role at an earlier stage, before there are any physiological changes, with a stimulus generally being processed cognitively by an individual before it produces an emotional response.

There has been recent theoretical controversy as to whether or not it is essential for such cognitive processing to precede an emotional or affective reaction. According to Zajonc (1984), "affect [emotion] and cognition are separate and partially independent systems and although they ordinarily function conjointly, affect could be generated without a prior cognitive process" (p. 117). In contrast, Lazarus (1982) argued that "Cognitive appraisal (of meaning or significance) underlies and is an integral feature of all emotional states" (p. 1021).

Zajonc (1980) supported his theoretical position by reference to a number of studies in which stimuli, such as pictures, were presented for such a brief period of time they couldn't be consciously perceived or subsequently recognised. In spite of that, those stimuli tended to be chosen rather than equivalent new ones when subjects were asked to select the stimuli they preferred. This suggested to Zajonc that conscious cognitive processing of stimuli was not necessary to produce an emotional response to them.

However, making preference judgements to stimuli doesn't have much relevance to ordinary emotional experience. Even more importantly, Zajonc arrived at his conclusion by assuming that cognition must involve conscious awareness. In fact, most cognitive psychologists would argue that many cognitive processes occur below the level of conscious awareness, and none of the studies discussed by Zajonc eliminated the possibility that pre-conscious cognitive processes were involved.

According to Lazarus (1982), *cognitive appraisal* always precedes emotional responses. The cognitive process is divided into two parts: *primary appraisal*, in which the situation is evaluated as positive, stressful, or irrelevant to well-being; followed by *secondary appraisal*, in which the individual takes into account his or her resources for coping with the situation.

The importance of cognitive appraisal to emotion was shown in a number of experiments discussed by Lazarus (1966). In one study,

STANLEY WAS PROUD OF HIS ABILITY TO
RELATE TO THE MASTERS.

subjects were shown a film of an accident in which a board caught in a
circular saw drives through the midsection of a worker, who then dies
writhing on the floor. Providing subjects with a suitable cognitive appraisal (such as telling them those involved in the film were actors)
considerably reduced the emotional impact of the film as assessed by
psychophysiological measures.

## How many emotions?

Another major issue in the psychology of emotion relates to the number
and nature of different emotions that can (or should) be identified—and
there is very little agreement among psychologists on this issue. One
reason for this is the lack of concordance among the cognitive, physiological, experiential, expressive, and behavioural components of emotion. A
much greater variety of emotional states can be identified at the experiential level, for example, than at the physiological level. Another reason is
that theorists differ in terms of whether they want to produce a general

theory emphasising the similarities among emotions, or a more specific theory in which dissimilarities are of major interest.

Auke Tellegen (1985) proposed a very general theory of emotion based on two independent or unrelated dimensions of *positive affect* (pleasant mood) and *negative affect* (unpleasant mood). Each dimension runs from low to high, and the crucial assumption is that virtually all emotional states can be understood within this two-dimensional framework (see below). For example, Tellegen accepts that anxiety and depression are separate emotional states; but focuses on the idea that they are similar emotions, in that high negative affect is involved, with the difference between them stemming from the fact that depression is associated with a lower level of positive affect than anxiety.

It may seem strange to regard positive and negative affect as independent dimensions rather than opposite sides of the same coin, but there is plenty of evidence that they are influenced by different factors. For example, as Tellegen pointed out, individuals high in *trait anxiety* (a predisposition to experience anxiety) experience much more negative affect than those low in trait anxiety, but an individual's level of trait

Tellegen's theory
of emotion (1985).

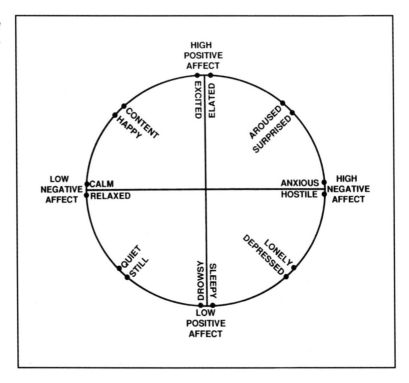

anxiety has no effect on his or her experience of positive affect. In similar fashion, extraverts experience more positive affect than introverts, but the two groups do not differ in the amount of negative affect experienced.

Other psychologists have argued that there are a relatively small number of major or primary emotions—the set proposed by Ekman and Friesen (1975) is reasonably representative. They studied facial expressions in several different cultures, and claimed there are six emotions which are expressed in the same way in all of them: happiness; surprise; anger; disgust; sadness; and fear. The obvious limitation of this approach is that there may be emotions that are not expressed in a clear way on the face.

In sum, there is no definitive answer to the question of the number and nature of emotions experienced by humans. However, it is reasonable to assume that there are approximately six to ten major emotions. There are similarities as well as dissimilarities among these emotions; as a consequence of these similarities, it is possible to relate them to a simple two-dimensional framework such as the one proposed by Tellegen.

# Summary

- The concept of *motivation* relates to the processes involved in starting, sustaining, and ending goal-directed behaviour.
- Some theorists divide motives into those which are *initiated internally* and those *initiated externally*; others distinguish between *cyclic* and *non-cyclic* motives; still others distinguish between *primary* or *unlearned* motives and *secondary* or *learned* ones.
- There is some merit in all these approaches, and they overlap with each other to some extent (e.g. cyclic motives tend to be triggered by internal factors).
- Early theories of motivation (such as *homeostatic drive theory* and *drive-reduction theory*) emphasised the physiological processes involved; whereas more recent theories (such as *intrinsic motivation theory* and *goal theory*) focus on cognitive processes in motivation.
- The study of *emotion* is complex, and emotional states need to be considered in terms of their cognitive, physiological, expressive, behavioural, and experiential components.

- A major theoretical problem is that the five components tend to show a lack of *concordance*.
- The *James-Lange theory* argued that our experience of emotion depends on preceding bodily changes, whereas the *Cannon-Bard theory* claimed that emotional experiences and bodily changes are independent.
- According to Schachter and Singer's *cognitive labelling theory*, emotional experience depends on physiological arousal and on the labelling or interpretation of that arousal.
- The contemporary view is that the cognitive aspect of emotion is of particular importance, because some form of *cognitive appraisal* of a stimulus typically occurs before an emotional state is experienced.

# Research methods 5

## The nature of science

### Changing views of science

It may seem reasonably straightforward to identify the main characteristics of science. However, the fact that there have been considerable changes in the conceptualisation of science during the twentieth century suggests that matters are more complex than you might think.

In essence, the traditional view of science was of *objective* gathering of data through observation and experimentation, with these data forming the basis for *generalisations* which lead on to theoretical accounts. This view was largely discredited by twentieth-century philosophers of science. For example, Karl Popper (1972) argued that scientific observation is much less objective than is generally thought, and demonstrated this by telling his audience: "Observe!" Their natural reply was to ask the question, "Observe what?", because people don't observe without some idea of what

they are looking for. Observation is thus always influenced by more or less explicit theories rather than being completely objective.

Popper is perhaps best known for his claim that the distinguishing characteristic of science is *falsifiability* rather than generalisation. A theory based on generalisations from numerous previous experiments (e.g. reward or positive reinforcement always facilitates performance) may prove to be wrong when tested tomorrow. In other words, generalising or extrapolating from what has been found to be true in the past can be dangerous, and we cannot prove conclusively that a theory is correct. In contrast, any good scientific theory is potentially falsifiable——it is possible to imagine experimental findings that would disprove the theory.

What are the implications of changing views of science for experimentation in psychology? Basically, philosophers of science have successfully demonstrated that the traditional view was unrealistic, and it is now accepted that scientific progress can occur in a number of different ways which don't conform to the rigid dictates of the traditional view. This change from rigid to flexible views of science corresponds to changes within psychology: psychologists have developed several different research methods for testing their scientific theories.

Most psychologists agree with Popper that experimental observations of behaviour should be interpreted within the context of an explicit or implicit theory. A theory provides a general explanation or account of certain phenomena, and also generates a number of *hypotheses* (testable predictions). For example, a general theory of anxiety might lead to the hypothesis that anxiety will slow down the rate of learning. Most experiments in psychology are designed to test one or more hypotheses: an essentially infinite number of experiments could be carried out, and it would be extremely difficult to decide which experiments were worth doing in the absence of any guidance from hypotheses and theories.

So far we have emphasised the way in which theories and hypotheses guide the choice of experiment and help to determine which aspects of behaviour are measured. However, it is important to note that there is a two-way traffic between theory and behavioural data: theories influence the aspects of behaviour that are measured, and behavioural data influence the development of theory. If the findings from an experiment appear to falsify the theory it was designed to test, then this may lead to revision or even abandonment of the original theory.

According to Kuhn (1970), the relationship between theory and data is rather more complicated than has generally been assumed. He argued that any given scientific discipline is dominated by a *paradigm* (general theoretical orientation) which is accepted by the great majority of scientists. This paradigm accounts for the findings that scientists regard as being of central importance; findings that do not fit with the prevailing paradigm are often ignored or treated as spurious.

What has been described so far is what Kuhn (1970) called the *normal mode* of science. However, as the evidence against the current paradigm increases, it becomes clear that a major theoretical shift is required. Then there follows a period of *revolutionary mode* science, in which the old paradigm is overthrown. Eventually, most of the evidence accounted for by the old paradigm is re-interpreted and integrated into a new paradigm, and science reverts to the normal mode. An example is the Copernican revolution, where the old Ptolemaic view that the planets and the sun revolve around the earth was replaced by our present view that the earth and the other planets revolve around the sun.

The most common way in which scientists (including psychologists) attempt to test their hypotheses is by means of experiments. Although this is frequently the most effective method available, the history of science demonstrates very clearly that scientific progress does not necessarily depend on carrying out laboratory experiments. Consider, for example, the science of astronomy. In spite of the fact that astronomers generally don't carry out experiments in the normal sense, they have been able through careful observation to obtain much valuable information about the nature of the universe.

In similar fashion, many important issues in psychology cannot be examined under laboratory conditions. For example, those who have been exposed to traumatic events (events causing a powerful shock) such as a major accident or kidnapping, sometimes subsequently develop a condition known as *post-traumatic stress disorder*. It is very important for psychologists to try to understand the processes triggering this disorder, but it would be completely unacceptable in ethical terms to attempt to produce this disorder under experimentally controlled conditions.

## Goals of science

What are the goals of science? As Malim et al. (1992) pointed out, three of the main goals are as follows:

1. *prediction;*
2. *understanding;*
3. *control.*

The theories formed by scientists permit them to make predictions or hypotheses about what will happen in situations that they have not previously investigated. For example, psychologists such as Thorndike discovered that animals could be persuaded to behave in certain ways if their behaviour was followed by reward or reinforcement. This led them to predict that the same would be true of the human species. The success or otherwise of predictions stemming from a theory are of great importance: any theory that generates numerous incorrect predictions must be seriously flawed.

Even if a theory generates a large number of accurate predictions, it does not necessarily follow that we will have a good understanding of what is happening. For example, a theory of memory proposed by Craik and Lockhart (1972) included the prediction that memory will be better for material that has been processed in terms of its meaning than for material that has not. Although this prediction has been confirmed experimentally several times, the precise reasons why it is beneficial to process meaning still remain unclear.

After prediction and understanding have been achieved, it is often possible to move on to control. For example, Thorndike, Skinner, and others predicted (and found) that people tend to repeat behaviour that is followed by reward or positive reinforcement, and the principles of operant conditioning were put forward in an attempt to understand what is going on. It is also possible to use reinforcement to control human behaviour, as when parents persuade their children to be well behaved in return for sweets.

## Scientific assumptions

As we saw in Chapter 3, many scientists have argued that science must be based on the assumption of *determinism*. In other words, everything that happens has a definite cause. It used to be assumed by determinists that it would prove possible to make very accurate scientific predictions about phenomena when their causes had been identified. However, there is growing recognition that many scientific phenomena are so complex that accurate prediction may never be possible. This complexity is perhaps especially great in psychology.

Popper (1972) argued persuasively that the observations made by scientists are by no means as objective as used to be thought. However, scientists still assume that the data they collect should be as objective as possible. One way of achieving this is for the experimenter to rely on data that are not affected by his or her own characteristics. Suppose, for example, that the reaction time of a participant in an experiment is being measured. Use of a timing apparatus that is initiated by the presentation of a stimulus and stopped by the participant's response produces a reasonably objective measure of the reaction time. In contrast, if the experimenter recorded reaction time by means of a stop watch, then the time recorded would depend on the speed of the experimenter's reactions as well as on those of the participant. In this latter case, objectivity would be lost. The notion that science should proceed on the basis of reasonably objective observation and measurement is often known as *empiricism*.

It sometimes happens that two scientific theories are both able to account for a range of observations. Which theory is to be preferred? One good way of deciding between them is to devise an experiment for which the two theories make different predictions. Whichever theory predicts the results of that experiment more accurately is preferable. Sometimes, however, it is not possible to think of a suitable experimental test. In that case, scientists invoke the *law of parsimony*: the more parsimonious theory (the one making fewer assumptions) is to be preferred if there are no other good grounds for making a decision.

All scientific theories contain a number of concepts. For example, Einstein's theory of relativity includes the concepts of "energy" and "mass". Each scientific concept should be as clearly defined as possible, and it should be possible to measure it with some precision. Scientific concepts that satisfy these criteria are said to have *operational definitions*. For example, psychologists have provided an operational definition of intelligence, claiming that it is what is measured by intelligence tests. If a concept lacks an operational definition, then it is difficult to know what it means, and scientists are likely to measure it in rather different ways.

# Major theoretical positions in psychology

In the great majority of scientific disciplines, nearly all of those people actively involved in research are firm believers in the scientific method and its various goals and assumptions. Psychology is exceptional in that there have been various prominent theoretical schools whose adherents have rejected some (or even most) of the major aspects of the scientific method. There is insufficient space here to consider all the major theoretical positions in psychology with respect to their adherence (or non-adherence) to scientific principles. Instead, three highly influential approaches will be discussed.

## Psychoanalysis

The psychoanalytic approach to psychology originated with Sigmund Freud (1856–1939), but was subsequently developed by Alfred Adler, Carl Jung, and numerous others. Psychoanalysis is mainly concerned with the treatment of neurotic patients suffering from a variety of anxiety disorders. As was pointed out in Chapter 2, Freud argued that most neuroses stem from unresolved conflicts and traumata (powerful shocks) going back to childhood. Anxiety-laden information about these conflicts is stored in the unconscious mind, and is not normally accessible to the conscious mind. In order for the patient to recover, it is necessary for him or her to gain *insight* (conscious understanding) of these conflicts.

Freud had a scientific background (having been trained in medicine) and he always claimed to adopt a scientific approach in his psychoanalytic theories. In fact, the reality is rather different if we relate what he did to the various scientific assumptions and goals discussed earlier in this chapter. Freud did not pursue the scientific goal of prediction with any vigour, in part because he did not carry out any experiments. However, he certainly followed the goal of understanding, in that he was very interested in trying to establish the deep-seated reasons why neurotic individuals behaved as they did. He was also interested in the goal of control, arguing that neurotic behaviour would be much reduced when the neurotic individual gained insight into his or her problems.

Freud was a strong believer in determinism. He argued that a major cause of neurosis was to be found in the experiences of childhood. He even argued that trivial phenomena such as missing an appointment with someone, calling someone by the wrong name, or humming a particular tune had definite causes to be found in the individual's motivational system. Freud (1961) suggested that in cases of failure to meet others as agreed, "the motive is an unusually large amount of contempt for other people" (p. 157).

The most obvious way in which Freud did not adhere to normal scientific procedures was in his failure to collect reasonably objective measures from his patients. He generally obtained information from his patients during unstructured therapy sessions. This involved relying on patients' reports of their conscious experiences, which could not be checked for accuracy, and which may have been influenced by what Freud had previously said to the patient.

Freud also failed to conform to the law of parsimony. He produced an enormous number of theoretical ideas over a 50-year period. Indeed, in some cases, he was able to use two or three different theories to explain some aspect of a patient's behaviour!

Freud rarely provided operational definitions of his theoretical constructs. For example, broad concepts such as the id, ego, and superego cannot be defined with precision, and can be measured only indirectly.

In sum, Freud's psychoanalytic approach represents an interesting mixture of the scientific and the non-scientific. However, the ultimate verdict must be that his is an unscientific approach. It fails Popper's falsifiability criterion, in that it is rarely clear if there are any possible observations which would lead to the overthrow of any of Freud's theories. This view is supported by the fact that very few experiments appearing to disprove Freudian views have been reported in the 60 or more years since they were originally proposed.

## Behaviourism

One of the main reasons why behaviourism was so influential was because it represented the first systematic attempt to make psychology a rigorous experimental science (see Chapter 2). The entire behaviourist approach was based on the notion of empiricism, with outright rejection of non-objective information such as that provided by introspection. The approach also adhered to the law of parsimony. As we saw in Chapter 2, the behaviourists claimed that even complex behaviour could be understood in terms of simple stimulus–response links. Indeed, a common criticism of behaviourism is that it was excessively parsimonious, often failing to do justice to the richness of human behaviour.

Behaviourism also conformed to the scientific assumption of determinism, and typically made use of operational definitions. The behaviourists argued that behaviour, in the form of responses, is caused by previous environmental stimuli, and this provided a deterministic framework for nearly all of their research. An emphasis on stimuli and responses was also found in most of the concepts used by behaviourists, based on the assumption that operational definitions of concepts in psychology can best be achieved by relating such concepts to observable stimuli and responses. For example, John Watson (the founder of behaviourism) argued that thinking is merely sub-vocal speech. Very few psychologists would accept this definition of thinking, but it does illustrate the way in which the behaviourists tried to devise ways of measuring apparently elusive concepts.

Although behaviourism was very successful in applying the scientific methods of the established sciences to psychology, it was extremely limited in many ways. Much that is important in human functioning (such as attention, imagery, and thinking) simply cannot be measured directly by focusing on observable stimuli and responses. As a consequence, the behaviourists tended to apply powerul scientific methods to simple phenomena such as the salivation of dogs or the lever presses of pigeons.

## Humanism

Carl Rogers and Abraham Maslow developed a major approach to psychology which is generally known as humanistic psychology. As was discussed in Chapter 2, humanistic psychologists argue that there are great advantages in the phenomenological approach (based on conscious experience) compared with more allegedly "scientific" approaches. According to Rogers (1959, p. 133):

> This personal, phenomenological type of study—especially when one reads all of the responses—is far more valuable than the traditional "hard-headed" empirical approach. This kind of study, often scorned by psychologists as being "merely self-reports", actually gives the deepest insight into what the experience has meant.

As the quotation makes clear, the humanistic approach does not adhere to the scientific method. Humanistic psychologists fully accept the importance of understanding, but are relatively unconcerned about prediction and control. Humanistic psychologists do not carry out formal experiments, and are thus not in a position to make specific predictions about human behaviour. The notion of control is rather alien to the humanistic approach, because it implies the systematic use of external forces to force people to behave in a particular way. In contrast, the whole humanistic focus is on internal factors, and particularly the self-concept.

Humanistic psychologists argue that people exercise choice in their behaviour, and they specifically deny that people's behaviour is at the mercy of outside forces. As a consequence, the humanistic psychologists are strong believers in free will and are opposed to the notion of determinism. Their reliance on people's reports of their conscious experiences means they are opposed to empiricism, because an individual's conscious experience is not open to inspection by others. Most humanistic psychologists use a relatively restricted range of theoretical assumptions and concepts, so there is reasonable adherence to the law of parsimony.

The position of humanistic psychologists with respect to the use of operational definitions is mixed. Rogers devised various measures for the self-concept. The most used is the *Q-sort method* or technique, in which several cards containing statements are sorted into categories on the basis of how well each statement describes the individual concerned. The same approach can be used to assess the ideal self, with the sorting being done in terms of how accurately each statement describes the individual as he or she would like to be. Although use of the Q-sort method provides operational definitions of the self-concept and of the ideal self, it is rather limited in some ways. For example, the individual sorting the cards can distort the results so as to appear to be more socially desirable than is actually the case.

There is no adequate operational definition of Maslow's concept of the need for self-actualisation. A rather indirect approach was used by Maslow (1962). He argued that one characteristic of self-actualisers is that they have peak experiences, during which they feel ecstatically happy and content. Maslow (1962) interviewed several people in an attempt to identify the features of peak experiences, and the kinds of factors which produced them. However, informal interviews do not provide a satisfactory objective measure of a complex concept such as self-actualisation.

## Should psychology be a science?

A psychologist and her friend were walking down a street one night when they saw a thief running down the road. The thief was startled to see them, threw the stolen jewellery he was carrying into some bushes, and ran off. The psychologist started looking for the jewellery under a nearby lamp-post. "Why are you looking there, when the jewellery was thrown into the bushes?" asked the psychologist's friend. "I am looking here, because here I can see what I am doing", replied the psychologist.

We can relate this story directly to the behaviourist approach. The behaviourists discovered it was easier to use the powerful light provided by the scientific method to study relatively trivial phenomena such as animal learning than to study phenomena of central importance such as consciousness, language, or creativity. In other words, they were looking in the wrong place for a full understanding of complex human behaviour.

In contrast, those following the psychoanalytic and humanistic approaches have investigated major aspects of human functioning, including our conscious experience of the world, our deepest strivings, the nature of the self-concept, and disabling emotional experiences. It would be extremely valuable to arrive at a complete understanding of all these phenomena, but this simply has not been possible by use of the scientific method. For example, it seems extraordinarily difficult to think of an experiment that would allow us to study in detail the need for self-actualisation.

In some ways, the differences between the scientific approach advocated by the behaviourists and the alternative approaches advocated by the psychoanalysts and the humanists resemble the contrast between the nomothetic and idiographic approaches discussed in Chapter 3. The behaviourists adopted the nomothetic approach, and wanted to establish general laws. In contrast, the psychoanalysts and humanistic psychologists were (and are) mainly concerned with the clinical treatment of individuals, and thus tend to be closer to the idiographic approach.

A reasonable conclusion about the respective merits of the scientific/nomothetic and the non-scientific/idiographic approaches was proposed many years ago by Falk (1956). He argued that the nomothetic approach favoured by the behaviourists is of particular value with respect to the scientific goals of prediction and control, whereas the idiographic approach of the psychoanalysts and humanistic psychologists may be of particular value with respect to the scientific goal of understanding. In other words, behaviourism, psychoanalysis, and humanistic psychology may all make valuable but different contributions to psychology.

Finally, it should be noted that some experts doubt whether psychology should be regarded as a mature science. For example, Kuhn (1962) claimed that all mature sciences have a paradigm or general theoretical orientation which is subscribed to by nearly all the researchers in any given discipline. The fact that there are (or have been) fundamental disagreements among behaviourists, psychoanalysts, and humanistic psychologists suggests that psychology doesn't possess a paradigm in Kuhn's sense. According to Kuhn, psychology is a pre-science rather than a science. That may be a somewhat harsh judgement on psychology, but Kuhn was surely right to point to the lack of consensus among psychologists on the issue of the best approach for psychologists to adopt.

# The experimental method

## Experimental variables

Most experimental research starts with a psychologist thinking of an *experimental hypothesis*—a prediction of what will happen in a given situation. For example, a possible experimental hypothesis is to say loud noise will have a disruptive effect on task performance. As with most hypotheses, this refers to a *dependent variable*, which is some aspect of behaviour; in this case, some measure of task performance. Most experimental hypotheses state that the dependent variable will be affected systematically by some specified factor, known as the *independent variable*; in this case, it is the intensity of noise. The independent variable is usually some aspect of the experimental situation that is manipulated by the experimenter.

It might be argued that we don't really need to go to the trouble of carrying out an experiment to decide whether loud noise disrupts task performance. We could compare the performance of workers in two factories, one of which is considerably noisier than the other. However, this approach is problematic in a number of ways. Suppose we discovered that the work performance of those in the noisier factory was inferior to that of those working in quieter conditions. This would not prove noise had a detrimental effect: perhaps those working in the noisier factory are less skilled than those in the quieter factory; or perhaps the working conditions are more difficult in ways other than the level of noise (such as too hot or too cold). We wouldn't be able to pinpoint the reasons for the difference in work performance in the two factories.

It is fundamentally important to the experimental method to avoid any *confounding variables*—variables that are manipulated along with the independent variable, and which prevent the results of experiments from being interpreted. If the workers in the noisier factory were less skilled than those in the quieter factory, skill level would be a confounding variable. Perhaps the greatest advantage of the experimental method is that it permits the researcher to eliminate confounding variables.

In spite of this, those using the experimental method aren't always successful in their efforts to avoid the presence of confounding variables. Consider, for example, a study by Jenkins and Dallenbach (1924), in which they gave a learning task to a group of subjects in the morning and then tested their memory for the material later in the day. The same learning task was given to a second group of subjects in the evening, and their memory tested the following morning after a night's sleep. Memory performance was considerably better for the second group, and Jenkins and Dallenbach argued that this was due to there being less interference with memory when people are asleep than when they are awake. Can you see the flaw in this argument? The two groups learned the material at different times of day, and so time of day was a confounding variable. Subsequent research by Hockey, Davies, and Gray (1972) indicated that the time of day at which learning takes place is much more important than whether or not the subject sleeps between learning and the memory test.

## Causality

Use of the experimental method potentially allows for *replicability*. If an experiment has been conducted in a carefully controlled fashion, it should be possible for other researchers to replicate or repeat the findings obtained from that experiment. The findings from any given experiment may be due to chance, or mistakes on the part of the experimenter, so replicating or repeating findings is extremely useful in establishing that they are genuine.

As Gross (1987) pointed out, one of the advantages commonly claimed for the experimental method is that it allows us to establish *cause and effect relationships*. In the terms we've been using, the independent variable in an experiment is often regarded as a cause, and the dependent variable (an aspect of behaviour) is the effect. Philosophers over the centuries have argued whether or not causality can definitely be established by experimentation, but the general opinion is that causality can only be inferred. If $y$ (e.g. a headache) always follows $x$ (e.g. a sharp blow on the head), then it is reasonable to draw the inference that $x$ causes $y$.

The reason for cautiousness about causality can be illustrated by considering an example in which it would be easy to draw an invalid causal inference. An experiment on malaria is carried out in a hot country, involving half the subjects sleeping in bedrooms with the windows open and the other half sleeping in bedrooms with the windows closed. Those sleeping in rooms with the windows open are found to be more likely to catch malaria. Having the windows open or closed is relevant to catching the disease, but it tells us nothing directly about the major causal factor in malaria (i.e. infected mosquitoes).

The experimental method can be used either for laboratory experiments or for field experiments carried out under more naturalistic conditions. As the strengths and weaknesses of the two kinds of experiment are rather different, it is often useful to carry out both laboratory and field experiments to investigate a given issue. If comparable results are obtained, we can have reasonable confidence that the findings haven't been distorted by limitations of the experimental setting.

## Laboratory experiments

The great majority of experiments in psychology are carried out in the laboratory, but psychologists differ enormously in their evaluation of the usefulness of laboratory experiments.

At one extreme, Boring argued: "The application of the experimental method to the problem of mind is the great outstanding event in the history of the study of the mind, an event to which no other is comparable". In contrast, Nick Heather (1976, pp. 31-33) was very dismissive of laboratory experimentation:

> Psychologists have attempted to squeeze the study of human life into a laboratory situation where it becomes unrecognisably different from its naturally occurring form … Experiments in psychology … are social situations involving strangers, and it might be suggested that the main kind of knowledge gleaned from years of experimentation with human subjects is information about how strangers interact in the highly artificial and unusual social setting of the psychological experiment.

Some of the major strengths and weaknesses of laboratory research can be clarified by looking at two different kinds of validity. *Internal validity* refers to the validity of research within the confines of the context in which it is carried out, whereas *external validity* means the validity of research outside the research situation itself.

Laboratory research is usually high in internal validity: the large degree of control over the environment which can be achieved in the laboratory tends to produce findings that are replicable or repeatable. However, it has often been argued that most laboratory experimentation is rather low in external validity, meaning we cannot be confident that what is true in the laboratory is also true of everyday life. The term *ecological validity* is often used to refer to the appropriateness of generalising from the laboratory to everyday settings.

It is obvious that much psychological research on humans lacks ecological validity to a greater or lesser extent. We spend most of our time interacting dynamically with our environment, deciding in which situations to put ourselves, and then responding to those situations as seems appropriate. Much of that dynamic interaction is typically lacking in laboratory research: the experimenter (rather than the subject) determines the situation in which the subject is placed, and what is of interest is the subject's response to that situation. As Silverman (1977) pointed out, "More often than not, the conclusions we draw from our laboratory studies pertain to the behaviour of organisms in conditions of their own confinement and control and are probably generalisable only to similar situations (institutions, perhaps, such as schools or prisons or hospitals)" (p. 108).

Ecological validity is also often lacking because laboratory experiments don't lend themselves to openness or self-disclosure on the part of the subjects. Subjects in experiments are usually rather wary, and unwilling to give away too much about themselves. As Jourard (1969) noted, "Man certainly does not live much of his life in relation to high status anonymous strangers, before whom he conceals most of his experience; his behaviour under usual laboratory conditions is perhaps generalisable to that aspect of his life" (p. 111).

Psychological experimentation often lacks ecological validity in other ways; in particular, many of the phenomena studied in the laboratory are of rather little relevance to everyday life. For example, consider the so-called *Sternberg paradigm*, in which subjects first memorise between one and six items (e.g. digits), followed shortly by the presentation of a test item. The task involves deciding as quickly as possible whether the test item is the same as one of the memorised items. The decision time lengthens as the number of memorised items increases, which presumably tells us something about the retrieval of information from short-term memory. But in spite of the fact that over one hundred experiments involving the Sternberg paradigm have been carried out, there is remarkably little

"MAKE A NOTE, SMALLWICK; 'DAY ONE:-SUBJECT EXHIBITED MILD ANXIETY SYNDROME.'"

evidence that the findings tell us anything of interest about the functioning of memory in everyday life.

Psychologists have become increasingly concerned about ecological validity in human research. Changing approaches to human memory (see Gillian Cohen, 1989, for a detailed account) illustrate how they have responded to the challenge of carrying out research that is relevant to everyday life, but which nevertheless is based on the experimental method.

Even comparatively recently, Neisser (1978) was able to argue that most laboratory research on humans had told us practically nothing about everyday memory. Generations of subjects had been asked to memorise lists of words, and a considerable amount was discovered about the factors (such as speed of presentation, word familiarity, and word imageability) influencing memory performance. However, it was not clear that the task of learning lists of words resembled everyday memory in any important way.

One of the main ways in which memory researchers have attempted to improve the ecological validity of their work is by designing laboratory experiments so that the task and conditions more closely resemble those of everyday life. A well-known example is the research of Elizabeth Loftus

(1979) on eyewitness testimony. Some of her experiments involve the presentation of a series of slides or film of an incident (such as a car accident), followed by questions or information that may affect memory for the incident. Finally, there is a memory test for the original incident. The main finding is that eyewitness recollection of the incident is very easily distorted by questions asked after the incident has taken place.

For example, Loftus and Palmer (1974) showed subjects an incident in which two cars hit each other. Although there was no broken glass, subjects who were asked "About how fast were the cars going when they smashed into each other?", were quite likely to report having seen broken glass. In contrast, when "contacted" or "hit" replaced "smashed" in the question, far fewer subjects claimed to have seen any broken glass.

How much ecological validity is there in this research on eyewitness testimony? The viewing of the incident by subjects sitting comfortably and paying close attention to it obviously differs considerably from that of most eyewitnesses in everyday life. However, if eyewitness testimony can be greatly distorted even when an incident has been observed under almost perfect viewing conditions, it is highly probable that it can be at least as distorted in everyday life. The use of post-incident questioning to distort eyewitness testimony probably corresponds all too well to what happens in everyday life.

Although the issue of ecological validity is probably the greatest problem with laboratory research, various other related problems beset experimenters working in the laboratory. It is important to note, however, that some of these problems can also affect field experiments and studies involving correlational designs.

## Experimenter bias

One of the potential problems with experimental research in psychology is that the experimenter nearly always has a clear idea of the results he or she expects to obtain; and these expectations may have subtle influences on subjects' behaviour. These influences are known as *experimenter bias*, a term suggested by Robert Rosenthal (1967).

Perhaps the first systematic demonstration of experimenter bias involved a horse known as Clever Hans. This horse was apparently able to count, tapping its hoof the appropriate number of times when asked a simple mathematical question. The psychologist Pfungst was able to show that the experimenter unconsciously made slight movements when the horse had tapped out the correct number, and Clever Hans was simply using these movements as the cue to stop tapping!

In the 85 years or so since the case of Clever Hans, there have been numerous demonstrations of experimenter bias. In one well-known study discussed by Rosenthal (1967), experimenters were instructed to count the number of head turns and body contractions made by flatworms. Before the experiment started, they were told that they should expect a lot of activity from half of the worms, but very little activity from the others. In fact, worms were assigned at random to the two groups, so there was no reason for assuming they would differ in activity level. Despite this, the experimenters reported twice as many head turns and three times as many body contractions in the worms that were allegedly highly active as in the "inactive" ones!

Proper application of the scientific method would involve all the subjects in an experiment being treated in precisely the same way; but Rosenthal obtained evidence that much psychological research doesn't achieve this goal. He discovered, for example, that male experimenters were more pleasant, friendly, honest, encouraging, and relaxed when their subjects were female than when they were male. Such findings led Rosenthal to conclude: "Male and female subjects may, psychologically, simply not be in the same experiment at all".

There is no doubt that experimenter bias does occur, and that steps should be taken to minimise such bias. One possibility is a *double blind* procedure, in which neither the experimenter working with the subjects

"...DEVOID OF ALL HUMAN BIAS...THIS PROGRAM IS, ESSENTIALLY, IDIOT PROOF..."

nor the person handling the experimental data knows the experimental hypothesis (or hypotheses) being tested. Although the double blind procedure reduces the possibility of experimenter bias, it is often too expensive and impractical to use. However, the incidence of experimenter bias is probably less than it used to be, for the very simple reason that more and more experiments involve subjects interacting with computers rather than with human experimenters.

## Demand characteristics

As we have seen, a persistent criticism of laboratory research is that the situation is so artificial that subjects behave very differently from the way they do normally. An amusing example of this was discussed by Guy Claxton (1980). He considered a standard laboratory task, in which subjects have to decide as quickly as possible whether sentences such as "Can canaries fly?" are true or false. Under laboratory conditions, people perform this task uncomplainingly. However, as Claxton (1980) pointed out, "If someone asks me 'Can canaries fly?' in the pub I will suspect either that he is an idiot or that he is about to tell me a joke".

Why do people behave in special ways under laboratory conditions? An important part of the answer lies in the fact that subjects actively try to work out the experimenter's hypothesis, and then act accordingly. Thus, in Claxton's example, subjects may feel the experimenter is testing their intelligence on the basis of how quickly they can answer the questions, and this construction of the situation stops them from responding as they would in a pub.

The American psychologist Orne (1962) has emphasised the importance of what he termed *demand characteristics*, which are "the totality of cues which convey an experimental hypothesis to the subjects". Demand characteristics include "the rumours or campus scuttle-butt about the research, the information conveyed during the original situation, the person of the experimenter, and the setting of the laboratory, as well as all explicit and implicit communications during the experiment proper". (In case you are wondering, the word "scuttle-butt" means gossip.) Orne's basic idea is that most subjects do their best to comply with what they perceive to be the demands of the experimental situation, but their perception will often be inaccurate.

Sometimes the demand characteristics in an experiment are so powerful that subjects can be persuaded to do some very strange things. In one experiment, subjects spent several hours adding numbers on random number sheets, then tearing up each completed sheet into at least 32 pieces. Presumably they construed the situation as a test of endurance, and this motivated them to keep going!

Some information about the demand characteristics in any given experimental setting can be obtained by the simple expedient of asking subjects to describe in detail what they felt the experiment was about. Armed with this information, the experimenter can take steps to ensure that the results of future experiments are not adversely affected by demand characteristics.

There is a further problem with demand characteristics, applying to subjects who have previously been involved in an experiment where they were deceived about the experimental purpose. As a result of such an experience, subjects tend to respond in the opposite direction to the one suggested by an experiment's demand characteristics.

Why should this be so? Silverman, Shulman, and Wiesenthal (1970, p. 210) observed this phenomenon, and explained:

> Deceived subjects may have become so alerted to possible further deceptions that they tend to respond counter to any cues regarding the experimenter's hypothesis. An element of gamesmanship may enter the experimental situation in that subjects become wary of 'tricks' underlying the obvious, and do not want to be caught in them.

## Evaluation apprehension

Rosenberg (1965) pointed out that an important aspect of most subjects' behaviour in the experimental or laboratory situation is what he called *evaluation apprehension*. He defined this as "an active anxiety-toned concern that he (the subject) win a positive evaluation from the experimenter or at least that he provide no grounds for a negative one". An illustration of the power of such evaluation apprehension is seen in a study by Rosenberg (1969), in which subjects were asked to rate their liking of 15 people from their photographs. Some subjects had been told that most people tended to like the photographs, whereas others were informed most people disliked them. This information had the predicted effect of making the subjects' ratings largely positive or negative, respectively.

For some of his subjects, Rosenberg (1969) attempted to increase evaluation apprehension by giving them the following information before they did the rating task: "Those photographs comprise a recently developed Test of Psychological Maturity. The pattern of responses given to these photographs by psychologically mature undergraduate students has been shown to be significantly different from the responses of those manifesting psychological maladjustment". This information produced a substantial increase in the tendency to like the photographs if most people allegedly liked them, or to dislike them if most people disliked them. Presumably this occurred because the subjects were very anxious to make sure that the experimenter didn't regard them as suffering from "psychological maladjustment!"

It could be argued that the main reason why subjects comply with the demand characteristics of experimental situations is because of their evaluation apprehension; and this is undoubtedly true in some experiments. However, the evidence suggests the need for favourable personal evaluation is generally more important than the need to comply with demand characteristics.

For example, Sigall, Aronson, and Van Hoose (1970) carried out an experiment on copying telephone numbers, in which the experimenter told subjects doing the test for the second time that he expected them to perform it at a rate that was actually slower than their previous performance. Adherence to the demand characteristics would lead to slow performance, whereas evaluation apprehension and the need to be capable would produce fast times. In fact, the subjects performed faster than they had done before, indicating the greater importance of evaluation apprehension.

"OI!...THE SCRIPT STOOPID,...WHAT ABOUT THE SCRIPT?!!..."

This conclusion was strengthened by the findings from a second condition, in which the experimenter not only said that he expected the subjects to perform at a relatively slow rate, but also told them that those who rush are probably obsessive-compulsive. The subjects given those instructions performed the task slowly, because they wanted to be evaluated positively.

## The "implacable" experimenter

In everyday life, our behaviour usually has some impact on the situation in which we find ourselves at any given moment. If we are having a conversation with someone, we expect what we say to produce some kind of reaction in that person. In other words, the situation normally influences our behaviour, and in turn our behaviour influences the situation. This can be contrasted with the standard experimental situation, in which the experimenter manipulates some aspects of the situation to observe their effects on the subject, but the subject's responses have a minimal impact on the situation.

Wachtel (1973) coined the term *implacable experimenter* to describe the typical laboratory situation, in which the behaviour of the experimenter is intended to occur independently of the subject's behaviour. There are at least two serious problems with experiments using an implacable (unyielding) experimenter.

First, because the situation is allowed to affect the subject but the subject isn't allowed to affect the situation, it is likely that the effects of situations on our behaviour are greatly over-estimated. Second, because much of the richness of the dynamic interactions between individual and situation has been omitted, there is a real danger that seriously over-simplified accounts of human behaviour will emerge.

## Samples and populations

Experiments in psychology rarely use more than about 100 subjects, but the experimenter nearly always wants his or her findings to be applicable to a much larger group. In technical terms, the subjects used in an experiment constitute one or more *samples* drawn from some larger *population*.

Thus, for example, an opinion poll may ascertain the voting intentions of 1000 British people (the sample), but it is assumed that what they say can be extrapolated to the entire population of Britain. However, in order for this to be true, it is essential for the sample to be representative of the population. In this example, we would obviously have no faith in the findings if all of those questioned lived in Brixton or Belgravia.

Unfortunately, the samples often used in psychological research aren't very representative. An analysis of published research in three leading

American journals some years ago revealed that the subjects in almost 80% of the studies were students. As students account for only 3% of the adult population of the United States it cannot be claimed that the samples generally used were at all representative. Very similar findings emerged from a survey of articles in two British research journals, with students used in 76.4% of non-clinical studies of adults.

It is undesirable for so much of the research in psychology to involve unrepresentative samples. Students tend to be younger and more intelligent than the adult population in general, and so will typically perform at a higher level on intellectually demanding tasks. However, it is less clear that students differ substantially from the general adult population in the nature of their psychological processes. In other words, the non-representativeness of most experimentation in psychology poses problems for the interpretation of findings, but the magnitude of the problem has not been established.

In recent years, psychologists have carried out fewer experiments on students and more experiments on various special groups within society. For example, cognitive neuropsychologists study brain-damaged patients to understand the organisation of human cognition; developmental psychologists investigate children of different ages; and clinical researchers study various clinical groups, such as anxious or depressed patients. So it is becoming less true every year that our knowledge of human behaviour is based almost entirely on the study of students.

Similar problems about the representativeness of samples have been encountered in research on other species; indeed, this factor may have played an important role in the development of learning theories in the 1920s and 1930s. Studying the learning skills of rats, Clark Hull and his associate Kenneth Spence argued in essence that rats simply learn which responses to make to the various stimuli provided by the learning environment (such as a maze). In contrast, Edward Tolman claimed rats engage in exploratory behaviour and acquire "cognitive maps" containing detailed information about the spatial layout of the environment.

Jones and Fennell (1965) took descendants of the rats used by both Spence and Tolman, and trained both groups to run along an eight foot U-shaped runway. The rats descended from those used by Spence paid very little attention to their environment, and were soon running rapidly along the runway. On the other hand, the rats descended from Tolman's animals engaged in a lot of exploratory behaviour and consequently ran considerably slower. It thus appears that the theoretical differences between Tolman and Spence owed much to their use of different strains of rat. Both Tolman and Spence made the mistake of assuming that what was true of their particular strain of rats would be true of other strains of rats.

## Field experiments

As an approximate statement, the strengths and weaknesses of *field experiments* are the opposite of those in laboratory experiments. More specifically, whereas laboratory experiments tend to be high in internal validity but low in external validity, field experiments are usually low in internal validity but high in external validity. The low internal validity results from the difficulty in achieving full control over real-life situations, and in choosing which subjects will take part in the experiment; the high external validity arises from observing behaviour unobtrusively under naturalistic conditions.

The fact that subjects in field experiments are often unaware that their behaviour is being observed conveys a number of advantages. In particular, many of the problems associated with much laboratory research (such as evaluation apprehension and demand characteristics) are either reduced or eliminated. As Silverman (1977) pointed out, "Virtually the only condition in which a subject in a psychological study will not behave as a subject is if he does not know he is in one" (p. 107).

As an example of a field experiment, consider a study by Lance Shotland and Margaret Straw (discussed in more detail by Eysenck & Eysenck, 1989), which was designed to establish some of the factors determining whether onlookers will intervene in a violent quarrel. They arranged for a man and a woman to stage an argument and fight fairly close to a number of bystanders. In one condition, the woman screamed, "I don't know you"; in a second condition she screamed, "I don't know why I ever married you!" When the bystanders thought the fight involved strangers, 65% of them intervened, against only 19% when they thought it involved a married couple. In other words, people are less likely to lend a helping hand if it is a "lover's quarrel" than when it is not. The bystanders were convinced that the fight was genuine, as was shown by the fact that 30% of the women were so alarmed that they shut the doors of their rooms, turned off the lights, and locked their doors.

A second example of a field experiment is provided by Nancy Jo Felipe and Robert Sommer (see Eysenck & Eysenck, 1989, for more details), who were interested in the notion that no-one likes strangers to come too close to them and invade what is known as their *personal space*. They arranged for a female experimenter to sit down very close to female college students in a reasonably empty university library. Thirteen per cent of the students ignored this threat to their personal space, but 70% left the library within 30 minutes. But although nearly all the students disliked having their personal space invaded, they were very reluctant to complain; only one out of 80 students asked the person sitting next to them to move away.

Could these field experiments on bystander intervention and personal space not have been carried out under laboratory conditions? They could, but there are various reasons to choose the field option: staging a violent quarrel in a laboratory, for example, would probably have appeared very artificial. The results of the experiments would also probably have been distorted if the subjects had been aware they were taking part in an experiment, because this would have prevented them from behaving in a natural fashion.

There is an ethical issue with many field experiments, including the two just described. It is normal ethical practice for an experimenter to ensure that he or she has the informed consent of subjects before they take part in an experiment; and by their very nature, most field experiments do not lend themselves to doing this. This may not cause a problem with entirely innocuous experiments, but the subjects who were frightened by being exposed to a staged violent quarrel could reasonably have complained about their treatment.

## Field observations

For some purposes, it is possible to make use of *field observations* rather than field experiments. The distinction between the two is that field experiments involve at least partial control by the researcher over the situation; whereas field observations merely involve the researcher observing the behaviour of people as they go about their everyday lives.

An interesting cross-cultural field observation study was carried out by Sidney Jourard. He watched pairs of people talking in cafes, and noted down the number of times one person touched another at one table during one hour. In San Juan, the capital of Puerto Rico, the total number of touches was 180. In contrast, the total in Paris was 110, and in London it was 0. Although this was a small-scale study, it offers interesting insights into cultural differences, and perhaps supports the notion that the English are cold and aloof.

Field observations are useful in other situations, such as investigations into traffic accidents. Observations of young children walking down streets can probably shed some light on why boys are far more likely than girls to be injured in car accidents; and observation of motorists' behaviour at notorious accident "black spots" can be informative about the environmental factors that play a part in causing accidents.

The main problem with field observations is in interpreting the findings. For example, the kinds of people who go to cafes in San Juan, Paris, and London may be quite different, and it is entirely possible that those who spend much of their time in cafes are by no means representative of the populations in question. As a consequence, it would be unwarranted to draw sweeping conclusions about cross-cultural differences in the liking for physical contact from these field observations.

## Correlational designs

The distinction between experimental and *correlational designs* can be seen if we consider a concrete example. Suppose an experimenter wants to test the hypothesis that watching violence on television leads to aggressive behaviour. An experimental study designed to test this hypothesis might involve dividing subjects randomly into two groups, one of which would be required to watch several violent television programmes, whereas the other wouldn't watch any violent programmes. The two groups could then be compared with respect to measures of behavioural aggression.

In contrast, a correlational study wouldn't involve any attempt to control the number of violent programmes watched by the subjects. Instead, the focus would be on a possible association between the number of violent programmes the subjects chose to watch, and some measure or measures of their level of aggression. There would be some support for the hypothesis if these two variables were found to be associated or *correlated* with each other.

Correlational designs are generally regarded as inferior to experimental designs, because it is difficult (or impossible) to establish cause and effect. In our example, the existence of an association between the amount of television violence watched and aggressive behaviour would certainly be consistent with the hypothesis that watching violent programmes can cause aggressive behaviour. However, there are other possible interpretations of the data. The causality may actually operate in the opposite direction: aggressive individuals may choose to watch more violent television programmes than those who are less aggressive. There may be a third variable which accounts for the association between the two variables of interest (watching violent programmes and aggressive behaviour). For example, people in disadvantaged families may watch more television programmes of all kinds than those in non-disadvantaged families, and their deprived circumstances may also cause them to behave aggressively. If that were the case, the number of violent television programmes watched might have no effect at all on aggressive behaviour.

Despite the interpretive problems posed by the findings of correlational studies, there are several reasons why psychologists continue to use this method. First, many hypotheses cannot be examined directly by means of experimental designs: for example, the hypothesis that smoking causes a number of physical diseases cannot be tested by forcing some people to smoke and forcing others not to smoke! All that can be done is to examine associations or correlations between the number of cigarettes smoked and the probability of suffering from various diseases.

Second, it is often possible to obtain large amounts of data on several variables in a correlational study much more rapidly and efficiently than would be possible using experimental designs. Use of a questionnaire, for example, would permit a researcher to investigate the associations between aggressive behaviour and a wide range of activities (such as watching violent films in the cinema; reading violent books; being frustrated at work or at home).

Third, interpretive problems are much reduced if there is no association between two variables. For example, if it were found there was no association at all between the amount of violent television watched and aggressive behaviour, this would provide fairly strong evidence that aggressive behaviour is not caused by watching violent programmes on television.

Fourth, the interpretive problems with associations or correlations between two variables are often not as great as in the example of violent programmes and aggression. Suppose, for example, we discover a correlation between age and happiness, in which older people are generally less happy than younger people. Although it wouldn't be possible to offer a definitive interpretation of this finding, we could be entirely confident that unhappiness does not cause old age!

## Single-case studies

The overwhelming majority of research in psychology has involved the use of experimental or correlational methods on groups of subjects. This approach permits the use of statistical techniques providing information about the extent to which the results obtained from a given sample can be generalised to some larger population.

However, there are sometimes good reasons why it is not feasible to use several subjects in a study. For example, a busy clinician or therapist may find the behaviour of a particular patient to be especially revealing, but have no possibility of collecting information from other patients suffering from the same problem. In such circumstances it can be very useful to carry out a case study, in which an individual patient is investigated thoroughly. Of course, there can be problems in trying to generalise from one patient to other patients, but case studies can provide valuable evidence about psychological disorders, and suggest theoretical ideas for subsequent testing.

Some researchers have gone further, and argued that the study of individual cases is often more fruitful than the study of groups of individuals. Those who favour this argument tend to adopt the idiographic rather than the nomothetic approach (see Chapter 3).

Gordon Allport is a well-known advocate of single-case studies, and in 1962 he proposed a relationship between the individual and generalisations about human behaviour (Allport, 1962, p. 407):

> Why should we not start with individual behaviour as a source of hunches (as we have done in the past) and then seek our generalisations (also as we have in the past) but finally come back to the individual not for the mechanical application of laws (as we do now) but for a fuller and more accurate assessment than we are now able to give? ... We stop with our wobbly laws of generality and seldom confront them with the concrete person.

Although many of those who advocate single-case studies are of an idiographic and sometimes of an anti-scientific persuasion, there has been a great increase in enthusiasm for the systematic investigation of individuals in recent years. For example, the behaviourist B.F. Skinner (1966) in a discussion of research on instrumental conditioning argued, "instead of studying a thousand rats for one hour each, or a hundred rats for ten hours each, the investigator is likely to study one rat for a thousand hours" (p. 21).

To clarify the ways in which single-case studies can contribute to psychological knowledge, it is worth considering some actual examples. A case study that proved a fertile source of theoretical ideas was carried out by Sigmund Freud on Dr Schreber, a lawyer suffering from paranoia (a mental disorder characterised by delusions). As Colman (1988) pointed out in his excellent discussion of this case, Freud was puzzled by the fact that paranoid patients tend to exhibit a number of apparently unrelated delusions—including a jealous feeling that their spouses or lovers have been unfaithful to them, the erroneous belief that people are plotting against them, the belief that several members of the opposite sex are in love with them, and delusions of grandeur.

Freud's discussions with Dr Schreber led him to an analysis of paranoia. According to Freud, homosexual desires underlie paranoia; but, because homosexuality tends to be viewed with disfavour by society, these desires remain unconscious and become distorted in various ways. One such distortion is for a male paranoiac to think his wife or lover loves another man, rather than the paranoiac loving another man himself, and this produces jealousy. Another distortion is for the paranoiac to think he loves many women rather than another man; however, because this is also unacceptable, it is further distorted into the notion that many women love the patient. A different distortion is to turn "I love a man" into the very different "I hate men"; again, the unacceptability of this thought can lead to the further distortion "Men hate me". Finally, delusions of grandeur are accounted for by assuming that a further distortion, in which "I love a man" is turned into "I love no-one", and then "I love no-one but myself".

Freud's account of paranoia based on a case study sounds rather (or very!) far-fetched, and is probably not correct in all its details. However, as Colman (1988) indicates, there is both clinical and experimental support for the view that repressed homosexuality is often of central importance in paranoia. In one study, words relating to homosexuality were presented very rapidly, and paranoiacs were faster than other people to recognise these words.

The case study of Dr Schreber indicates clearly that clinical case studies can provide powerful theoretical ideas. However, it also demonstrates that supplementary clinical and experimental evidence is usually required before the conclusions of a case study are generally accepted.

## Case studies in cognitive neuropsychology

Case studies have also been used extensively within cognitive neuropsychology, which is concerned with the cognitive functioning of brain-damaged patients. The basic claim of cognitive neuropsychologists is that observing what brain-damaged patients can and cannot do will help us understand how the cognitive system is organised in normal individuals. For example, Shallice and Warrington (1970) discovered a brain-damaged patient, KF, had good long-term memory but very poor short-term memory. These findings strengthened the argument for separate long-term and short-term memory systems.

It is increasingly argued that single-case studies are of more value than group studies in cognitive neuropsychology. Caramazza and McCloskey (1988) went so far as to argue that: "Valid inferences about the structure of normal cognitive systems from patterns of impaired performance are only possible for single-patient studies" (p. 519).

What are the problems with carrying out experiments comparing, for example, a group of acquired dyslexic individuals (brain-damaged patients experiencing reading problems) with a group of normal individuals? In essence, the argument is that the substantial differences in brain damage from one patient to the next make it virtually impossible to form a group of patients showing the same pattern of cognitive impairment. Forming an artificial group of subjects out of patients with different kinds of brain damage and with different cognitive problems confuses rather than clarifies matters.

The value of individual case studies in cognitive neuropsychology can be illustrated by the work of Campbell and Butterworth (1985). They were interested in the idea that we read familiar words by using stored information about their pronunciation, but we use an entirely different process to read unfamiliar words and non-words. They discovered a student who had no difficulty in saying unusual but familiar words such as "placebo" and "idyll", but who found it extremely difficult to say even simple non-words such as "bant". This case study strongly suggests that the processes involved in saying familiar and unfamiliar words or non-words are different.

What are the limitations of single-case studies in cognitive neuropsychology? A major limitation is that case studies are unlikely to be informative in the absence of an adequate theoretical framework. Campbell and Butterworth had a theory of reading which predicted there would probably be some patients who found it very much more difficult to say non-words than familiar words, and this theoretical context allowed them to appreciate the significance of their findings. In addition, we can have more confidence in the value of their case-study data because they are consistent with a well-established theory.

Another limitation of the case-study approach in cognitive neuropsychology is that the cognitive system of the brain-damaged patient may have differed before brain damage in some important way from those of the great majority of normal individuals. In that case, it would obviously be dangerous to use the data from such a patient to draw conclusions about normal cognitive functioning.

Finally, a brain-damaged patient may respond to brain damage by developing compensatory strategies, designed to overcome at least some of the impairments produced by the damage. Such strategies may obscure the direct effects of brain damage on the cognitive system, and make it difficult to make sense of the findings.

The answer to most of these limitations of single-case studies is to carry out a number of such studies. If the same or similar findings are obtained in a number of individual patients, it is unlikely that they all had unusual cognitive systems prior to brain damage, or that they have all made use of the same compensatory strategies.

In sum, case studies can be very useful in terms of suggesting new theoretical ideas and in testing existing theories. Such case-studies are of particular value when supported by the findings from systematic experimental studies. The greatest danger of the case-study approach is that very general conclusions may be drawn on the basis of a single atypical individual; and for this reason it is important to have supporting evidence from other sources.

# Data collection

Regardless of the method used in any given study, numerous different kinds of data or dependent variables can be assessed for the subjects taking part.

The most common form of data collection consists of measuring some aspect or aspects of the subject's behaviour (such as the extent to which he or she co-operates with other subjects; or the speed with which he or she can solve a problem). For some purposes, it is useful to take various psychophysiological measures (such as heart rate or brain-wave activity). Other forms of data collection are based on self-report, including questionnaires and interviews. It is also possible to make use of archive material.

There is general agreement that behavioural observations and psychophysiological measures are both of considerable value in research; but there is less consensus concerning the value of other forms of data such as self-report, survey, and archive material.

## Self-report: Interviews and questionnaires

Common sense suggests a useful way of understanding an individual's behaviour is to ask him or her. Although the advantages of self-report may seem obvious, we saw in our discussion of introspection (Chapter 3) that people often have little or no conscious awareness of the factors leading them to behave as they do. However, self-reports are sometimes very informative. For example, almost everyone at an airport can provide accurate information about the reasons why he or she is there.

Two of the major forms of self-report are *interviews* and *questionnaires*, and their strengths and weaknesses tend to be complementary. In essence, interviews possess a certain amount of flexibility, and it is possible for misunderstandings to be resolved. However, they have the disadvantage that the data obtained may reveal more about the social interaction processes between the interviewer and the person being interviewed (the interviewee) than about the interviewee's thought processes and attitudes.

In contrast, questionnaires provide a consistent and structured assessment of an individual's personality, attitudes, and so on, without any contamination from an interviewer or other person. All subjects are asked the same questions, regardless of the suitability or relevance of particular questions to particular individuals.

A problem common to the data obtained from both interviews and questionnaires is *social desirability bias*. Most people want to present

CERTAIN ASPECTS OF THE QUESTIONNAIRE TRIED GAVIN'S CAPACITY FOR HONESTY.

themselves in the best possible light, so there is a danger they will provide socially desirable rather than honest answers to questions about themselves. This problem can be handled in the interview situation by a sensitive interviewer asking supplementary questions in order to establish the truth; the usual approach in questionnaire design is to include a *lie scale*. Lie scales contain questions to which the socially desirable answer is likely to differ from the honest answer (e.g. "Of all the people you know, are there any you actively dislike?"; "Do you ever talk about other people's private lives?"). Anyone who consistently answers such questions in the socially desirable direction is assumed to be lying, and his or her questionnaire data are discarded.

In view of the complementary strengths and weaknesses of interviews and questionnaires, there are strong arguments for attempting to combine the two approaches. Consider, for example, work on life events involving difficult changes within an individual's life (such as divorce or job loss). Many theorists have argued that several different kinds of negative consequences (such as anxiety, depression, or physical illness) can result from excessive life events. However, studies based on questionnaire assessment of life events (e.g. the Social Readjustment Rating Scale) have generally indicated rather small associations between life events and physical and emotional complaints.

The questionnaire approach to life events is flawed, because subjects often show poorer memory for life events that happened some time ago than for more recent events. In addition, most questionnaires do not permit proper assessment of the factors responsible for the life events or of the personal significance of any given life event (losing one's job, for example, is likely to be of much greater significance to a middle-aged person with a family to support than to someone who would shortly have retired anyway).

George Brown and Tirril Harris (1978) resolved many of these problems by giving their subjects very long interviews in which they asked numerous detailed questions structured rather like a questionnaire. However, their approach allowed the interviewer to pursue matters arising from the answers in order to clarify matters. This combination of interview and questionnaire revealed that life events can have a much greater impact on the development of depression and other complaints than had appeared from previous research.

## Survey methods

Several important issues in psychology can most appropriately be investigated by survey methods. For example, cross-cultural psychologists are interested in comparing different cultures, and this can be done by carrying out surveys in which numerous members of each culture are tested in some way. Survey methods are also used extensively within a single culture, and involve comparing different groups within society (e.g. the young versus the old; men versus women; various social classes).

Survey studies typically make use of questionnaires or interviews, administered to all the groups of interest. These questionnaires or interviews often measure attitudes, but can also assess personality, patterns of behaviour, and so on. A characteristic of many survey studies is that they require hundreds (or even thousands) of subjects; as a consequence, the questionnaires or interviews are generally designed to be completed relatively quickly and easily.

As an example of a survey study, Marjorie Lowenthal, Majda Thurher, David Chiriboga and their associates investigated the effects of age on happiness (this study is discussed in more detail by Eysenck, 1990). They studied four groups of people: students in their last two years at school; young newly-weds; middle-aged parents about 50; and those preparing for retirement, with an average age of 60. Questionnaires were used to assess happiness and well-being, and to decide whether individuals were high or low in terms of the number of their positive and negative experi-

"HAH! KIDS THESE DAYS ARE SO MOODY... I TELL YOU, IN OUR DAY, WHEN WE WERE MISERABLE...WE STAYED MISERABLE...!"

ences. The four groups differed relatively little in their overall levels of happiness; but the younger groups (students and newly-weds) were much more emotionally changeable than the older groups, and experienced more emotional highs and lows.

Because surveys generally involve interviews and / or questionnaires, they suffer from the problems of these self-report measures discussed previously. Another major problem with survey methods is ensuring the various samples used in the study are properly representative of the populations from which they come. This goal is often not attained. For example, Shere Hite used the survey method to obtain information about women's sexual experiences and feelings. Questionnaires were sent to abortion rights groups, women's groups, and women's centres on college campuses, and advertisements were placed in magazines. Not surprisingly, the 3000 women who responded were on average younger, better educated, and more feminist in outlook than most women. The non-representative nature of the sample meant the study couldn't provide information about most women's experiences and feelings.

Non-representativeness may also have been a problem with the study of Lowenthal et al. just described. It is possible that unhappy people were less likely than happy ones to agree to participate in their study, which would mean that all their groups would appear to be happier than they actually are.

The ideal solution to the problem of representativeness is random sampling, in which members of the population in question (such as young newly-weds) are selected at random to participate in the survey. However, attempts to produce true random sampling are generally rather expensive. In addition, the unavailability of complete listings of the relevant populations, and the probable refusal of many of those selected at random to take part, mean that proper random sampling is extremely difficult to achieve.

## Archive material

Archive material is a form of data primarily of value to social psychologists. Governments, polling organisations, political parties, and other groups collect large amounts of information about different sections of society; and this information, which is sometimes available in archival form, can be of value in testing psychological hypotheses.

An example of the use of archive material is a study by Hovland and Sears (1940). They wanted to test the frustration–aggression hypothesis, according to which frustration produces aggression. Drops in cotton prices in the United States were assumed to cause frustration and the number of lynchings was taken as a measure of aggression. As predicted, when archive material was studied, those years in which the cotton prices were lowest tended to be the ones with the most lynchings.

Archives have the advantage of having already been collected by other people, and therefore minimal effort is required to assemble the necessary data to test any given hypothesis. It is often also possible to investigate trends over long periods of time using such data, as in the study by Hovland and Sears. The most obvious disadvantage is that the archive material was usually collected for a purpose that differs considerably from that of the psychologist who subsequently uses it. As a consequence, data that would be of particular value in testing the psychologist's hypothesis or hypotheses may not be available.

The other major limitation of most archival material is that it is dificult to interpret. This point can be illustrated in the study by Hovland and Sears: although a low cotton price may have been frustrating for cotton producers, those who purchased cotton goods presumably found the reduced price anything but frustrating. Furthermore, Hovland and Sears basically obtained an association or correlation between cotton prices and the number of lynchings, and one cannot establish cause and effect with confidence on the basis of such evidence.

# Summary

- Views about the *nature of science* have changed during the course of this century; it is now generally accepted that scientists' observations are dictated by theory, and scientific theories and hypotheses can be falsified but not conclusively confirmed.
- The main goals of science include *prediction*, *understanding*, and *control*.
- Most scientists (but not all psychologists) believe in *determinism*, *empiricism*, the *law of parsimony*, and the use of *operational definitions* for concepts.
- The main kind of research in psychology involves the use of the *experimental method* under laboratory conditions, which has the advantages of avoiding *confounding variables*, permitting *replication* or repetition of findings, and allowing *cause and effect* to be inferred.
- Various problems beset laboratory research, including a lack of *ecological validity; experimenter bias; demand characteristics; evaluation apprehension;* the *implacable experimenter;* and *non-representative samples*.
- *Field experiments*, in which the experimental method is used in more naturalistic surroundings, have the advantage of greater ecological validity than is generally found in the laboratory; but experimental control is often poor, so it can be difficult to replicate findings.
- *Correlational designs* are used by psychologists to examine possible associations or correlations between two *variables*; they do not enable cause and effect to be inferred, but can provide rapid accumulation of large amounts of data.
- Many important issues (e.g. smoking and physical health) cannot readily be studied with experimental designs.
- Although the great majority of studies using experimental and correlational designs involve groups of subjects, there is growing interest in the use of *single-case studies*.
- Single-case studies can be very useful in suggesting guidelines for future research, and are particularly valuable when it is difficult to obtain *homogeneous groups* of subjects (e.g. in some clinical research).
- A great variety of data can be collected in psychological research: *behavioural observations* are the most commonly used form, but many psychologists collect *psychophysiological* or *self-report* data.
- Self-report data (e.g. *questionnaires* and *interviews*) are potentially valuable, but can be difficult to interpret because of *social desirability bias* and other problems.
- *Archive material* can also be useful, but can usually only be incorporated within a correlational design.

## Further reading

A readable account of alternative research methods is provided by A.M. Colman in *What is psychology? The inside story* (London, Hutchinson, 1988). Some of the problems with the experimental method are discussed in a lively fashion by N. Heather in *Radical perspectives in psychology* (London, Methuen, 1976).

# 6 The conduct of research

## Ethics and psychology

The work of scientists sometimes poses important ethical questions. For example, was it morally defensible for physicists to develop the atomic bomb during the 1940s? Can research on human embryos be justified? Should scientists participate in the development of chemical weapons that could potentially kill millions of people? All these questions about the ethics of scientific research are difficult to answer, because there are good reasons for and against each programme of research.

It is probably true to say there are more major ethical issues associated with research in psychology than in any other scientific discipline, for several reasons. First, all psychological experiments involve the study of living creatures (whether human or the members of some other species), and their entitlement to be treated in a caring and respectful way can be infringed by an unprincipled or careless experimenter.

Second, the findings of psychological research may reveal what appear to be unpalatable facts about human nature, or about certain groups within society. No matter how morally upright the experimenter may be, there is always the danger that extreme political organisations will use the findings to further their political aims.

Third, psychological research may lead to the discovery of powerful techniques that can be used for purposes of social control. It would obviously be dangerous if such techniques were to be exploited by dictators or others seeking to exert unjustifiable influence on society.

Psychologists have become increasingly concerned about ethical issues in recent years, and their deliberations have led to the development of consensual views (and some dissenting views) on the limits of acceptability in psychological research.

# The ethics of human experimentation

The human subject in a psychological experiment is in a rather vulnerable and exploitable position. As Kelman (1972) pointed out, "most ethical problems arising in social research can be traced to the subject's power deficiency" (p. 993).

The experimenter is often a person of fairly high status (such as a university researcher or professor), and he or she possesses expertise and knowledge about the experimental situation which is not shared by the participant. When an experiment takes place in the laboratory, the experimenter has the advantage of operating on "home ground", and the setting is almost entirely under his or her control. Finally, the acceptance of scientific research as an activity that is valued by society also enhances the position of power enjoyed by the experimenter.

The position of the subject, however, is often very different. He or she is generally of lower academic status than the experimenter, and will typically have only a partial understanding of the purpose of the experiment. As a result, the subject assumes the experimenter knows what he or she is doing, and so surrenders control of the experimental situation to him or her. This makes it unlikely that the subject will question what is being done, or to refuse to continue further with an experiment, even if he or she finds that what is involved is distasteful.

The lengths to which subjects will go to fulfil what they regard as their obligations to the experimenter were shown most strikingly by Stanley Milgram (1974). As we saw in Chapter 1, he found that approximately half his subjects were prepared to administer an extremely severe electric shock to another subject in a learning experiment when the experimenter told them that they must. This obviously shows a very high degree of obedience to the power and authority of the experimenter.

However, it should be noted that most of the participants didn't totally surrender responsibility to the

Top: the "shock box" from the Milgram "Obedience" experiment (1974); Middle: the shock box being explained to the subject; Bottom: the actor being wired up to the shock box. Photographs courtesy Mrs A. Milgram.

experimenter in an unthinking fashion. Many of those who obeyed the experimenter became extremely tense and uneasy as the experiment progressed, and were acutely aware of the moral dilemma into which they had been placed.

These are ethical problems which can occur while subjects are actually participating in an experiment, but such problems can also arise from the uses to which information gathered from an experiment is subsequently put. Those who plan and carry out research tend to come from the more powerful and influential groups within society, whereas those who act as subjects often come from weak and low-status groups. In at least some kinds of experiments, there is the danger that the knowledge obtained might be used to the disadvantage of those who supplied the data.

For example, consider the Moynihan Report (Rainwater & Yancey, 1967), which identified the disintegration of the Negro family as the most important barrier to Negroes' ability to achieve equality. The ethical problem here is that the findings could have been used to discourage politicians from taking action on other fronts (such as reducing inequalities in the distribution of resources).

## General principles

Because most ethical problems in research on humans stem from the subject being typically in a much less powerful position than the experimenter, it follows that steps need to be taken to ensure that the subject is not placed in a powerless and vulnerable position.

In general, the easiest method is to make sure the subject is told precisely what will happen in the experiment, before requesting that he or she give *voluntary informed consent* to take part. However, small children are obviously unable to provide informed consent, and there are some types of experiment in which deception is essential if the research is to take place at all. Deception is certainly widespread. Menges (1973) considered approximately 1000 experimental studies that had been carried out in the United States, and discovered that full information about what was going to happen was provided in only 3% of cases.

A well-known example of research involving deception is the work of Asch (1956). He gave subjects the task of deciding which one of three lines projected on to a screen was equal in length to a standard line. This task was done in groups of between four and eleven people, all but one of whom were stooge subjects working under instructions from the experimenter. The subjects gave their judgements one at a time, and the seating was arranged so that the genuine subject gave his or her opinion last. On key trials, all the stooge subjects gave the same wrong answer.

The aim of the experiment was to see whether the genuine subjects would conform to group pressure, and this did in fact happen in about one-third of the trials. But if the subjects had been told the experiment was designed to investigate conformity to group pressure, and that all the other subjects were stooges, the experiment would obviously have been pointless.

One possible reaction is to argue there should never be any deception in psychological experiments, even if it means some lines of research must cease. However, this ignores the fact that many forms of deception are entirely innocuous: for example, memory researchers are often interested in people's ability to remember information that they weren't explicitly trying to remember. This can only be done by deceiving the subjects as to the true purpose of the experiment until the memory test is presented.

Of course, other forms of deception are by no means so harmless. The study by Shotland and Straw (discussed in Chapter 5), in which subjects were led to believe they were witnessing a genuine violent quarrel, would be regarded by many people as unacceptable.

When is deception justified? There is no simple answer, but clearly a number of relevant factors need to be taken into consideration. First, the less potentially damaging the consequences of the deception, the more acceptable it is. Second, it is easier to justify the use of deception in studies that are important in scientific terms than in those that are trivial in nature. Third, deception is more justifiable when there are no alternative, deception-free, ways of investigating an issue.

One method of avoiding the ethical problems associated with deception is the use of *role-playing* experiments. In essence, subjects are asked to play the role of subjects in a deception experiment, but they are told beforehand about the experimental manipulations. Although this approach obviously eliminates the ethical problems of deception studies, it is not clear it is a satisfactory way of investigating behaviour. As Freedman (1969) pointed out, what we are likely to obtain from role-playing experiments are "people's guesses as to how they would behave if they were in a particular situation".

Another way of handling the deception issue was used by Gamson, Fireman, and Rytina (1982). They carried out an experiment in which the subjects were videotaped while they discussed what was allegedly a forthcoming court case. The experimenters made repeated efforts to persuade the subjects to argue for a point of view different to their own. Gamson et al. were interested in the extent to which the subjects would be willing to go along with these attempts at persuasion. Clearly the experiment could not be carried out without deception. In order to address the ethical issue over deception, Gamson et al. (1982) arranged for all of the potential subjects in the experiment to be telephoned beforehand, and asked whether they would be willing to take part in research in which they would be misled about its purpose until after it was over. Only those who indicated that they were willing were subsequently recruited for the experiment itself.

Whether or not an experiment involves deception, there are other important safeguards that should be built into virtually all experimentation on humans. It should be made clear to all the subjects at the outset that they have the *right to withdraw* from the experiment at any time. Furthermore, they do not have to say why they are withdrawing from the experiment if they choose not to. If subjects wish, they can also insist that the data that they have provided during the experiment should be destroyed. The right to withdraw, when coupled with voluntary informed consent, helps to ensure that those participating in research are not rendered powerless and vulnerable.

Although the right to withdraw is now standard practice, this was by no means the case in the past. Consider, for example, the research by Milgram (1974) on obedience to authority which was mentioned earlier in the chapter. When any of his subjects said that they wanted to leave the experiment or to stop administering electric shocks, they were told they had to continue with the experiment. Such attempts to force individual subjects to complete an experiment would no longer be permitted.

Another important safeguard in experimental research is *debriefing*. According to the *Ethical principles for conducting research with human participants* (published by the British Psychological Society in 1993):

> The investigator should discuss with the participants their experience of the research in order to monitor any unforeseen negative effects or misconceptions ... Investigators have a responsibility to ensure that participants receive any necessary de-briefing in the form of active intervention before they leave the research setting.

There are really two aspects to debriefing: (1) provision of information about the experiment, and (2) attempts to reduce any distress that may have been caused by the experiment. Milgram's (1974) research on obedience to authority provides a good example of how debriefing often works. At the end of the experiment, all the subjects were reassured that they had not actually administered any electric shocks. They then had a lengthy conversation with the experimenter and with the person who had apparently received the electric shocks. Those subjects who had obeyed the experimenter by being willing to administer severe shocks were told that their behaviour was normal, and that many others who had taken part in the experiment had also experienced feelings of conflict and tension. Subsequently, all of the subjects received a detailed report on the study.

The debriefing and other procedures used by Milgram (1974) seem to have been very successful. As many as 84% of the subjects stated they were glad to have taken part in the experiment, and only 1% expressed negative feelings about the experiment. Further questioning revealed that four-fifths of the subjects felt more experiments of this sort should be conducted, and 74% said they had learned something of personal importance as a result of taking part.

Another safeguard that is increasingly built into experimental research is that of *confidentiality*. The convention in psychology is for published accounts of research to refer to group means, but to withhold information about the names and performance of individuals. If the experimenter cannot guarantee anonymity, then this should be made clear to potential subjects beforehand. However, as Gross (1992) pointed out, there are very exceptional cases in which it is appropriate to ignore confidentiality. Suppose, for example, that the behaviour of a severely depressed patient in an experiment leads the researcher to suspect that he or she might commit suicide. It may then be necessary for the well-being of the patient to break the confidentiality rule.

An increasingly popular way of attempting to ensure psychological research is ethically acceptable is to set up *ethical committees*, which consider all research proposals from the perspective of the rights and dignity of the subject. The existence of such committees obviously helps to correct the power imbalance between experimenter and subject. However, an important issue is the membership of ethical committees: if all the members are researchers in psychology, they may be disinclined to turn down proposals from professional colleagues. For this and other reasons, it seems desirable for every ethical committee to include at least one non-expert member of the public.

In many countries, professional bodies of psychologists maintain an active involvement in ensuring all psychological research is ethically justifiable. For example, the British Psychological Society and the American Psychological Association have published detailed guidelines for the ethical conduct of research in Britain and the United States, respectively. These guidelines include several conditions designed to protect human subjects, including voluntary participation, informed consent, right to withdraw, privacy, and freedom from harm.

We have already mentioned the *Ethical principles for conducting research with human participants* (see page 148). These Principles should be followed by all researchers in the United Kingdom, including students

# Extracts from the British Psychological Society
## "Ethical Principles for Conducting Research with Human Participants"

### General

In all circumstances, investigators must consider the ethical implications and psychological consequences for the participants in their research. The essential principle is that the investigation should be considered from the standpoint of all participants: foreseeable threats to their psychological well-being, health, values or dignity should be eliminated.

### Consent

Whenever possible, the investigator should inform all participants of the objectives of the investigation.

Research with children or with participants who have impairments that will limit understanding and/or communication such that they are unable to give their real consent requires special safe-guarding procedures.

Where research involves any persons under sixteen years of age, consent should be obtained from parents or from those *in loco parentis*.

Investigators should realise that they are often in a position of authority or influence over participants who may be their students, employees, or clients. This relationship must not be allowed to pressurise the participants to take part in, or remain in, an investigation.

The payment of participants must not be used to induce them to risk harm beyond that which they risk without payment in their normal lifestyle.

### Deception

The withholding of information or the misleading of participants is unacceptable if the participants are typically likely to object or show unease once debriefed.

Participants should never be deliberately misled without extremely strong scientific or medical justification.

### Debriefing

Debriefing does not provide a justification for unethical aspects of any investigation.

Some effects which may be produced by an experiment will not be negated by a verbal description following the research. Investigators have a responsibility to ensure that participants receive any necessary debriefing in the form of active intervention before they leave the research setting.

### Withdrawal from the investigation

At the onset of the investigation, investigators should make plain to participants their right to withdraw from the research at any time, irrespective of whether or not payment or any other inducement has been offered.

### Confidentiality

Information obtained about a participant during an investigation is confidential unless otherwise agreed in advance.

### Protection of participants

Investigators have a primary responsibility to protect participants from physical and mental harm during the investigation.

Where research may involve behaviour or experiences that participants may regard as personal and private, the participants must be protected from stress by all appropriate measures, including the assurance that answers to personal questions need not be given.

In research involving children, great caution should be exercised when discussing the results with parents, teachers or others *in loco parentis*, since evaluative statements may carry unintended weight.

### Observational research

Unless those observed give their consent to being observed, observational research is only acceptable in situations where those observed would expect to be observed by strangers.

*The full text of this statement is available from the BPS, St Andrew's House, 48 Princess Road East, Leicester LE1 7DR.*

who carry out experiments as part of their course. The key to conducting research in an ethically acceptable fashion is expressed in the following way in the Principles: "The essential principle is that the investigation should be considered from the standpoint of all participants; foreseeable threats to their psychological well-being, health, values or dignity should be eliminated".

In the United States, every complaint against psychologists is investigated by the American Psychological Association's Committee on Scientific and Professional Ethics. If the complaint is found to be justified, then the psychologist concerned is either suspended or expelled from the Association.

## Ethical principles in therapy

The treatment of mental disorders poses a number of major ethical issues over and above those involved in ordinary research; moreover, these issues are of great importance, because the future lives of patients are involved. We don't have the space to deal with every aspect, but the provision of treatment for homosexuality raises some issues of central significance.

Many therapists have argued they have a responsibility to satisfy the needs of their clients; accordingly, if homosexuals request therapy to help develop a heterosexual orientation, it should be given to them. In other words, voluntary informed consent is all that is required for the treatment to proceed. However, other therapists have disputed whether homosexuals are really in a position to given such informed consent.

This point of view was articulated by Silverstein (1972, p. 4):

> To suggest that a person comes voluntarily to change his sexual orientation is to ignore the powerful environmental stress, oppression if you will, that has been telling him for years that he should change. To grow up in a family where the word "homosexual" was whispered, to play in a play- ground and hear the words "faggot" and "queer", to go to church and hear of "sin" and then to college and hear of "illness", and finally to the counselling centre that promises to "cure", is hardly [to live in] an environment of freedom and voluntary choice. The homosexual is expected to want to be changed and his application for treatment is implicitly praised as the first step toward "normal" behaviour.

Another ethical problem is that the very fact of providing treatment for homosexuality suggests it is regarded as a mental disorder, in the same way as schizophrenia or depression. This can increase homosexuals' feelings of being an oppressed minority.

These considerations have led some therapists to propose that no treatment should be offered to homosexuals even when they specifically request it. However, this poses the ethical issue that some homosexuals are so distressed by their sexual orientation they might be driven to suicide or some other desperate measure if they were denied the possibility of receiving treatment.

There is no easy solution to these complex ethical issues—it is clear there are valid arguments both for and against the provision of treatment for homosexuals. A reasonable compromise position is to regard treatment for homosexuality only as a last resort. It should be provided only for those homosexuals who are very distressed by their sexual orientation, and only when it appears no other solution is feasible. Every effort must be made to eliminate the idea that homosexuality should be thought of as a mental disorder. But even if this compromise position is adopted, there will still be cases in which it is very difficult to know whether or not treatment is justified.

## The use of animals in research

Before addressing the ethical issues involved in animal research, it is worth considering some of the reasons why psychologists have chosen to use animals in so many of their experiments. First, it is possible (although there are major ethical considerations) to carry out experiments on animals that simply would not be permissible with humans. Here are three examples: surgical procedures can be used to produce damage to specific parts of an animal's brain; animals can be used in controlled breeding programmes; animals can be exposed to prolonged periods of social or other forms of deprivation.

Second, the members of many species develop and reproduce over very much shorter time periods than do members of the human species. As a consequence, it is much more feasible to carry out studies focusing on the effects of either heredity or early experience on behaviour in such species.

Third, it is generally accepted that the human species is more complex than other species. It may, therefore, be easier to understand the behaviour of other species than that of humans. This makes animal research extremely useful, provided that we are willing to assume that other species are broadly similar to our own (see Chapter 2).

The most obvious problem with the use of animals in research is that many of the ethical principles which guide psychological research on human subjects cannot be applied. For example, it is impossible for animals to give voluntary informed consent to take part in experiments.

As a consequence, it is extremely important for psychologists to develop ethical guidelines to protect animal rights, and to prevent them from suffering or being exploited. In fact, most institutions regard the use of animals in research as such a sensitive matter that it is normal practice for all proposed animal experiments to be carefully considered by an ethical committee. In addition, in the United Kingdom, the Home Office has overall control: anyone who wants to carry out research must have a licence, and inspectors from the Home Office regularly inspect all animal facilities. All research on vertebrates in the United Kingdom is governed by the Animals (Scientific Procedures) Act of 1986. This Act contains numerous safeguards to ensure that vertebrate research is ethically sound. Finally, the British Psychological Society published guidelines on animal research in 1985. These guidelines state that researchers should "avoid, or at least minimise, discomfort to living animals".

The position one adopts on the issue of using animals in research depends on how similar to humans other species are seen to be. In a nutshell, it is much less reasonable to use animals in a wide range of experiments if they are rather similar to us (e.g. in that they experience things in the same way as we do) than if they are very different.

As we saw in Chapter 2, views on the similarity of our species to others have changed considerably over the centuries. At one extreme is the seventeenth-century philosopher René Descartes, who argued that animals are very much like machines, and lack the soul (with its powers of thinking) that is the supreme human characteristic. It follows from this position that animals are very much inferior to humans.

The views of Charles Darwin (1859) stand in stark contrast to those of Descartes. According to Darwin, the human species has evolved out of other species, and thus we are all members of the animal kingdom. It is difficult from the evolutionary perspective to cling to the notion that we are radically different from other species: we may be more intelligent, of course, but this is simply a matter of degree.

Darwin's (1872) work on emotions is of particular importance to the use of animals in research. He was impressed by the similarities in the expression of emotional states between humans and other species, and his findings suggest it might be very unwise to assume that animals do not experience emotions in approximately the same way that we do. We cannot be certain, however, because there is no way of knowing the emotional experiences of members of other species.

Many psychologists do not agree with Darwin that the human species is rather similar to other species. For example, humanistic psychologists such as Carl Rogers and Abraham Maslow argued that a key characteristic of humans is our need for self-actualisation, which involves full realisation of our potential in all ways. Other species lack this need, and focus instead on much more basic needs such as those for food, drink, and sex. Within the context of the humanistic approach, members of the human species are very different and considerably more complex than the members of any other species.

People nowadays differ considerably in their views about the acceptability of using animals in psychological research. Some argue that using animals for research involves exploitation, and so no such research should be undertaken. Others claim human welfare is so much more important than animal rights that we are justified in inflicting considerable suffering on animals if there is the prospect of helping mankind by so doing. As we are dealing with complex matters of ethics and morality, there can be no final answer.

Probably most people would reject the extreme view that animals should never be used in research, as well as the opposite extreme view that there should be no consideration of the suffering to which animals might be exposed in research. Malim, Birch, and Wadeley (1992) discussed some animal research that would probably seem acceptable to nearly everyone. One programme of research was designed to provide us with a better understanding of the behaviour of animals that damage crops. This research led to the development of much more effective scarecrows, so that other, far more unpleasant, methods of preventing crop damage (e.g. poison) no longer needed to be used. In this particular case, animal research actually served to produce a substantial reduction in animal suffering.

Another example of animal research that was apparently almost entirely beneficial was reported by Simmons (1981). Pigeons were carefully trained by means of operant conditioning to detect life rafts floating on the sea. Because the vision of pigeons is extremely good, their detection performance was considerably superior to that of helicopter crews: 85% detection compared to only 50%. In this case, animal research has undoubtedly enabled many human lives to be saved.

There is much animal research that most people would feel was much less justified than the examples we have just considered. A case in point is research within the cosmetics industry. Rabbits have eye make-up applied around their eyes in order to discover whether or not it causes irritation and inflamation of the eyes.

It is important when considering ethical problems to distinguish between *absolute morality* and *relative morality*. Immanuel Kant and other philosophers argued in favour of an absolute morality in which the ends cannot justify the means. In contrast, most people probably subscribe to a relative morality, according to which one judges the acceptability of actions in terms of the benefits that accrue.

Although the notion of an absolute morality may have some appeal, it tends to be inflexible and unrealistic in practice. For example, the moral principle "Always tell the truth" sounds very reasonable. However, if a madman with a gun demands to know where your mother is, it would make very little sense to adhere to the principle.

The alternative view that the ends can justify the means is favoured by most psychologists. It was expressed by the American Psychological Association Committee on Ethical Standards in Psychological Research as: "The general ethical question always is whether there is a negative effect upon the dignity and welfare of the participants that the importance of the research does not warrant".

The idea that decisions about the use of animals in research should be based on a consideration of the benefits and costs involved is sensible, and makes intuitive sense. Suppose, for example, a proposed experiment will involve inflicting considerable pain on several animals. This would surely seem less acceptable if the experiment were designed to produce improved cosmetics than if it were intended to lead to the development of treatment for a dreadful disease affecting humans.

In practice, however, there can be problems. First, it is often impossible to know what the benefits and costs of a piece of research are going to be until after the experiment has been carried out. Second, one person's assessment of the benefits and costs of a piece of research may not agree with someone else's. Third, there is the difficult matter of deciding how much suffering a given experimental procedure inflicts on an animal. As we cannot ask an animal directly what it is experiencing, we have to rely on its behaviour. However, this may be a misleading guide to its feelings. As Gross (1992) pointed out, what needs to be done is to find out as much as possible about each species. This will permit us to make more accurate interpretations as to the true significance of any form of behaviour.

Finally, it is worth broadening our discussion to consider the ways in which humans (other than psychologists) treat animals. There are three main areas of concern: meat production; ill-treatment of pets; and animals kept in captivity in zoos and circuses. There is increasing criticism in all three areas. So far as meat production is concerned, it seems cruel and immoral to many people that animals such as calves and chickens are kept in severely restricted conditions so that they can scarcely move. There is also growing concern that the methods of slaughtering used in abattoirs may involve much more suffering than is generally admitted by those involved in meat production.

The Royal Society for the Prevention of Cruelty to Animals is one of the main organisations concerned with ill-treatment of animals. Every year it deals with many thousands of cases of animals that have been starved, beaten, or ill-treated in other ways. Battersea Dogs Home in London receives many dogs every week that have simply been abandoned by their owners. There are indications that public concern at the ill-treatment of pets is growing, at least in terms of the amount of media coverage it commands.

Zoos and circuses have attracted more adverse publicity in recent years. It is felt that animals kept in captivity in relatively restricted and alien environments may suffer stress. There is also disquiet that many circus animals are degraded by being forced to perform unnatural tricks.

In sum, there is increased concern about the ways in which animals are treated. The growing focus on ethical issues in animal experimentation is part of a more general re-evaluation of our relationship with other species. Much remains to be done. However, there are encouraging signs that the rights of animals to humane treatment (whether inside or outside the laboratory) are being increasingly recognised.

## Psychology and social control

Psychologists and non-psychologists alike are concerned that our increased knowledge of human behaviour may be used by unscrupulous politicians and others to exercise social control over various groups within society. This was less true in the early days of psychology, when psychologists were sometimes remarkably willing to become involved in the process of social control.

A case in point is the attitude adopted by a number of American psychologists when intelligence tests were developed in the early years of this century. Between 1910 and 1920, several American states passed laws designed to prevent certain categories of people (including those of low intelligence) from having children. Psychologists often exerted pressure to have these laws passed: the prominent Californian psychologist Lewis Terman, for example, argued: "If we would preserve our state for a class of people worthy to possess it, we must prevent, as far as possible, the propagation of mental degenerates".

As a consequence of his views, and those of other psychologists, a Californian law of 1918 required all compulsory sterilisations to be approved by a board including "a clinical psychologist holding the degree of PhD". In similar fashion, pressure by psychologists helped persuade the state of Iowa to legislate in 1913 for "the prevention of the procreation of criminals, rapists, idiots, feeble-minded, imbeciles, lunatics, drunkards, drug fiends, epileptics, syphilitics, moral and sexual perverts, and diseased and degenerate persons".

Most psychologists nowadays would be very reluctant to be associated with such harsh measures. However, some psychologists in the second half of the twentieth century have advocated using psychological principles for purposes of social control, the most prominent being B.F. Skinner. His major contention was that nearly all behaviour is under the control of reward or reinforcement, with responses followed by reward increasing in frequency and those not followed by reward decreasing in frequency. This is known as *operant conditioning*. According to Skinner (1953), it follows that we can determine and control people's behaviour by providing the appropriate rewards at the appropriate times: "Operant conditioning shapes behaviour as a sculptor shapes a lump of clay".

There is no doubting the power of reward or reinforcement. For example, pigeons have been trained by reinforcement to perform unnatural actions like playing table tennis, and pigs have learned to dance and to play the piano. However, it is a long step from demonstrating that behaviour can often be shaped (or gradually shifted in a desired direction) by reinforcement to the idea that all behaviour is under the control of reinforcers. Most people believe much of their behaviour is freely chosen rather than solely determined by external rewards, but Skinner (1971) argued that "freedom" is simply the term we apply to behaviour when we are unaware of the reinforcers controlling it.

Critics of Skinner have argued that his approach seeks to deprive people of freedom and dignity, because their behaviour can be controlled by some other person who dictates the reinforcers or rewards to which they are exposed. Skinner's (1971) reply is that all behaviour is controlled by rewards anyway, and so the idea we are free to behave as we choose is an illusion. Furthermore, a society in which socially desirable behaviour was consistently rewarded would produce a better society than any currently in existence.

Some of these ideas are to be found in Skinner's earlier (1948) novel, *Walden Two*, which describes a Utopian (ideally perfect) community using Skinnerian principles to create an ideal society. The basic notion was that principles of behavioural engineering could be used to create a highly fulfilling environment. Skinner envisaged a high degree of external control in his ideal society, with children being reared mainly by child-rearing professionals, and government being by self-perpetuating committees rather than by elected representatives.

There are two major issues that need to be discussed here. First, is it actually true that all behaviour is controlled by reinforcement or reward, with the implication that an entire society could be transformed by the

B.F. Skinner, 1976
(From a preface
to a new printing
of *Walden Two*,
Macmillan:
New York.)

It is now widely recognized that greater changes must be made in [our] way of life. Not only can we not face the rest of the world while consuming and polluting as we do, we cannot for long face ourselves while acknowledging the violence and chaos in which we live. The choice is clear: either we do nothing and allow a miserable and probably catastrophic future to overtake us, or we use our knowledge about human behavior to create a social environment in which we shall live productive and creative lives and do so without jeopardizing the chances that those who follow us will be able to do the same.

application of conditioning principles? Second, is it ethically acceptable for psychologists to contemplate the kind of social control discussed in *Walden Two*?

## Behaviour modification

As far as the first issue is concerned, some of the main support for Skinner's view that human behaviour is determined by reinforcement has come from the use of *behaviour modification* to resolve behavioural problems and mental disorders.

This approach leans heavily on reinforcement principles, as can be seen in the case of a young child cured of excessive crying (Hart et al., 1964). Some of the child's crying was caused by physical pain, but most of it appeared to be reinforced or rewarded by the attention that the child received from its teachers. Crying that occurred because it was rewarded by attention was stopped by being ignored, because non-rewarded behaviour decreases in frequency and eventually ceases or extinguishes. When the teachers were instructed to begin to pay attention to the child again when it cried, the crying rapidly reappeared.

Reinforcement principles have been applied on a larger scale in institutions such as prisons and hospitals, in which *token economies* have been set up (see Chapter 2). In a token economy, people can earn tokens by behaving in appropriate ways, and can then exchange those tokens for some desired reward (such as cigarettes). These token economies have been found to produce desired changes in behaviour, but the effects are often disappointingly short-lived when an economy's members are no longer systematically rewarded.

The fact that maintaining an individual's behaviour requires the careful provision of reward for desired behaviour only and over a long period of time suggests that a dictator would find it enormously difficult to exercise such social control over an entire society.

Some of the limitations of Skinner's operant conditioning approach were noted by Breland and Breland (1961). They discovered that each species of animal tends to have characteristic ways of behaving, regardless of the nature of the training involved. For example, pigs tend to root before they start eating, whereas domestic fowl scratch the ground. They used the term *instinctive drift* to refer to such phenomena, and the important implication is that learning is limited by various biological constraints.

The importance of biological factors in conditioning was emphasised by Seligman (1970). He proposed the idea of *preparedness*, which refers to the fact that every species finds some kinds of learning much easier than others, because of their biological make-up. For example, it is natural for pigeons to peck for food, and so Skinner found that it was relatively easy to train pigeons to peck at coloured discs for a food reward.

Skinner seemed to favour the contrasting notion of *equipotentiality*, according to which virtually any response can be conditioned in any stimulus situation. The evidence against equipotentiality is overwhelming—for example, it would be extremely difficult to train an animal to run away from the sight of food in order to receive a food reinforcement!

One of the crucial limitations of Skinner's operant conditioning approach, as these criticisms illustrate, is that he exaggerated the importance of external determinants of behaviour and minimised the significance of internal factors (such as cognition, physiology, and inherited characteristics). Skinner (1971) indicated clearly the extent to which he felt we are controlled by the external environment: "The environment not only prods or lashes, it selects ... Behaviour is shaped and maintained by its consequences". His rejection of internal factors (sometimes known as the "empty organism" doctrine) is illustrated in his curt dismissal of physiology (Skinner, 1980): "A science of behaviour has its own facts ... No physiological fact has told us anything about behaviour that we did not know already".

The other fundamental limitation of Skinner's approach is that reinforcement or reward typically has a much greater effect on performance than it does on learning. For example, suppose someone offered you a reinforcement or reward of £1 every time you said, "The earth is flat". You might very well say it several hundred times. However, although the reward would have influenced your performance or behaviour, it is utterly improbable that it would also have affected your knowledge or learning to the extent you now believed the earth was actually flat. In similar fashion, the uprisings in Eastern Europe in 1989 showed that decades of forcing people to behave in certain ways hadn't really changed their underlying desires for freedom and democracy.

## The ethics of social control

As the available evidence suggests that reinforcement techniques probably cannot be used to control a society over long periods of time, the ethical issues concerning social control are of less vital concern.

However, there are clearly potential dangers in attempting to control the behaviour of members of a society. A crucial problem lies in the motivation of those responsible for behavioural control. If their motives are good, then the end result (as in *Walden Two*) may be desirable. On the other hand, no-one would want to see psychological techniques of behavioural control being applied to society by unscrupulous individuals seeking to impose their own wishes on other people.

# Summary

- Human participants in experiments are typically in a *vulnerable* position, and there are real dangers that some unprincipled experimenters may exploit their vulnerability.
- The appropriate way to redress the power balance between experimenter and subject is to ensure that subjects are given *full information* about what the experiment will involve, and to proceed with the experiment only after the subject has given his or her *voluntary informed consent.*
- Problems still arise, because some experiments require the subjects to be *deceived* about the purposes of the experiment.
- Safeguards to ensure that human research is ethical include the participants' *right to withdraw, full debriefing* at the end of the experiment, *confidentiality* of information about individuals, the use of *ethical committees,* and the publication of *ethical guidelines* by professional organisations.
- In the *treatment* of some conditions (such as homosexuality), there may be doubts as to whether proper voluntary informed consent can be given, because of the strong pressures exerted by society.
- Most *animal experiments* raise important ethical issues, because animals manifestly cannot provide voluntary informed consent to participate in an experiment.

- The best approach to these difficult problems seems to involve deciding whether the ends justify the means in terms of the likely benefits accruing from carrying out the experiment.
- Ethical issues are also raised by Skinner's *operant conditioning* approach based on the assumption that behaviour can be controlled by rewarding desired actions and not rewarding undesired ones.
- Skinner claimed it is both possible and desirable for psychologists to exercise *social control* over the members of society, and thus ultimately to create an ideal society, but critics have responded with horror to the apparent loss of freedom and dignity involved.
- It is not true that all behaviour is determined by external reinforcers or rewards, and so there is no real prospect of Skinner's reinforcement-controlled society coming about.

## Further reading

The ethical issues posed by experimental research are discussed in an interesting way by H.C. Kelman (1972) in The rights of the subject in social research: An analysis in terms of relative power and legitimacy, *American Psychologist, 27*, 989–1016. An up-to-date statement of appropriate rules for ethically acceptable research is the following: Ethical principles for conducting research with human participants. (1990), *The Psychologist, 3*, 270–272. There is a judicious account of the Skinnerian approach and its limitations in *Theories of learning* (5th ed.) by E.R. Hilgard and G.H. Bower (Englewood Cliffs, NJ, Prentice-Hall, 1981).

# References

Allport, F.H. (1924). *Social psychology.* Boston: Houghton Mifflin.

Allport, G.W. (1937). *Personality.* London: Constable.

Allport, G.W. (1962). The general and the unique in psychological science. *Journal of Personality, 30,* 405–422.

Allport, G.W. (1965). *Letters from Jenny.* New York: Harcourt, Brace & World.

Aronoff, J. (1967). *Psychological needs and cultural systems: A case study.* Princeton, NJ: Van Nostrand.

Asch, S.E. (1956). Studies of independence and conformity: A minority of one against a unanimous majority. *Psychological Monographs, 70 (416).*

Ayllon, T., & Azrin, N.H. (1968). *The token economy: A motivational system for therapy and rehabilitation.* New York: Appleton-Century-Crofts.

Bergin, A.E. (1971). The evaluation of therapeutic outcomes. In A.E. Bergin & S.L. Garfield (Eds.), *Handbook of psychotherapy and behaviour change: An empirical analysis* (2nd ed.). New York: Wiley.

Boring, E.G. (1929). The psychology of controversy. *Psychological Review, 36,* 97–121.

Bowers, K. (1973). Situationism in psychology: An analysis and a critique. *Psychological Review, 80,* 307–336.

Bowlby, J. (1953). *Maternal care and mental health.* Geneva: World Health Organization.

Breland, K., & Breland, M. (1961). The misbehaviour of organisms. *American Psychologist, 61,* 681–684.

Broca, P. (1865). Sur le siege de la faculté du langage articule. *Bulletin de la Société d'Anthropologie, 6,* 337–393.

Brody, N. (1988). *Personality: In search of individuality.* London: Academic Press.

Brown, G.W., & Harris, T. (1978). *Social origins of depression.* London: Tavistock.

Bruner, J.S., Goodnow, J.J., & Austin, G.A. (1956). *A study of thinking.* New York: Wiley.

Campbell, R., & Butterworth, B. (1985). Phonological dyslexia and dysgraphia in a highly literate subject: A developmental case with associated deficits of phonemic processing and awareness. *Quarterly Journal of Experimental Psychology, 37A,* 435–475.

Cannon, W.B. (1929). *Bodily changes in pain, hunger, fear, and rage* (2nd ed.). New York: Appleton-Century-Crofts.

Caramazza, A., & McCloskey, M. (1988). The case for single-patient studies. *Cognitive Neuropsychology, 5,* 517–528.

Carroll, J.B. (1986). Factor analytic investigations of cognitive abilities. In S.E. Newstead, S.H. Irvine, & P.L. Dan (Eds.), *Human assessment: Cognition and motivation.* Dordrecht: Nijhoff.

Cartwright, D.S. (1979). *Theories and models of personality.* Dubuque, Iowa: Brown Company Publishers.

Chomsky, N. (1959). Review of Skinner's "verbal behaviour". *Language, 35,* 26–58.

Christie, M.J., & Brearty, E.M. (1981). The laboratory environment, psychophysiology and psychosomatics. In G. Koptagel-llal & O. Tuncer (Eds.),

*Proceedings of the 13th European Conference on Psychosomatic Research.* Istanbul: University Press.

Claparede, E. (1911). Recognition et moité. *Archives de Psychologie, 11,* 75–90.

Clarke, A.M., & Clarke, A.D.B. (1976). The formative years? In A.M. Clarke & A.D.B. Clarke (Eds.), *Early experience: Myth and evidence.* London: Open Books.

Claxton, G. (1980). Cognitive psychology: A suitable case for what sort of treatment? In G. Claxton (Ed.), *Cognitive psychology: New directions.* London: Routledge & Kegan Paul.

Cohen, G. (1989). *Memory in the real world.* Hove: Lawrence Erlbaum Associates Ltd.

Colman, A.M. (1988). *What is psychology? The inside story.* London: Hutchinson.

Craik, F.I.M., & Lockhart, R.S. (1972). Levels of processing: A framework for memory research. *Journal of Verbal Learning and Verbal Behavior, 11,* 671–684.

Craske, M.G., & Craig, K.D. (1984). Musical performance anxiety: The three-systems model and self-efficacy theory. *Behaviour Research and Therapy, 22,* 267–280

Cronbach, L.J. (1957). The two disciplines of scientific psychology. *American Psychologist, 12,* 671–684.

Darwin, C. (1859). *The origin of species.* London: Macmillan.

Darwin, C. (1872). *Expression of the emotions in man and animals.* London: Murray.

Davis, S. (1976). The development of Isabelle. In A.M. Clarke & A.D.B. Clarke (Eds.), *Early experience: Myth and evidence.* London: Open Books.

Davison, G.C., & Neale, J.M. (1986). *Abnormal psychology* (4th ed.). Chichester: Wiley.

Davison, G.C., & Neale, J.M. (1990). *Abnormal psychology* (5th ed.). Chichester: Wiley.

Deci, E.L. (1971). Effects of externally mediated rewards on intrinsic motivation. *Journal of Personality and Social Psychology, 18,* 105–115.

Deci, E.L. (1975). *Intrinsic motivation.* London: Plenum.

Drever, J. (1964). *A dictionary of psychology.* Harmondsworth: Penguin.

Ekman, P., & Friesen, W.V. (1975). *Unmasking the face: A guide to recognizing emotions from facial expressions.* New York: Prentice-Hall.

Elkin, I., Shea, T., Imber, S., Pilkonis, P., Sotsky, S., Glass, D., Watkins, J., Leber, W., & Collins, J. (1986). *NIMH treatment of depression collaborative research program: Initial outcome findings.* Paper presented to the American Association for the Advancement of Science.

Ericsson, K.A., & Simon, H.A. (1980). Verbal reports as data. *Psychological Review, 87,* 215–251.

Ethical Principles for Conducting Research with Human Participants (1990). *The Psychologist, 3,* 270–272.

Eysenck, H.J. (1952). The effects of psychotherapy: An evaluation. *Journal of Consulting Psychology, 16,* 319–324.

Eysenck, H.J. (1966). Personality and experimental psychology. *Bulletin of the British Psychological Society, 19,* 1–28.

Eysenck, H.J., & Eysenck, M.W. (1989). *Mindwatching: Why we behave the way we do.* London: Prion.

Eysenck, M.W. (1984). *A handbook of cognitive psychology.* Hove: Lawrence Erlbaum Associates Ltd.

Eysenck, M.W. (1990). *Happiness: Facts and myths.* Hove: Lawrence Erlbaum Associates Ltd.

Eysenck, M.W., & Keane, M.T. (1990). *Cognitive psychology: A student's handbook.* Hove: Lawrence Erlbaum Associates Ltd.

Falk, J.L. (1956). Issues distinguishing idiographic from nomothetic approaches to personality theory. *Psychological Review, 63,* 53–62.

Fechner, G.T. (1860). *Elemente der Psychophysik.* Springer: Berlin.

Ford, D.H., & Urban, H.B. (1963). *Systems of psychotherapy: A comparative study.* New York: Wiley.

Freedman, J.L. (1969). Role playing: Psychology by consensus. *Journal of Personality and Social Psychology, 13,* 107–114.

Freud, S. (1961). *The psychopathology of everyday life.* Translated by A. Tyson. New York: W.W. Norton.

Funkenstein, D.H. (1955). The physiology of fear and anger. *Scientific American, 192,* 74–80.

Galton, F. (1869). *Hereditary genius.* London: Macmillan.

Galton, F. (1876). Théorie de l'hérédité. *La Revue Scientifique, 10,* 198–205.

Gamson, W.B., Fireman, B., & Rytina, S. (1982). *Encounters with unjust authority.* Homewood, IL: Dorsey Press.

Gray, J.A. (1985). A whole and its parts: Behaviour, the brain, cognition and emotion. *Bulletin of the British Psychological Society, 38,* 99–112.

Gross, R.D. (1987). *Psychology: The science of mind and behaviour.* London: Hodder & Stoughton.

Gross, R.D. (1992). *Psychology: The science of mind and behaviour* (2nd ed.). London: Hodder & Stoughton.

Guilford, J.P. (1936).Unitary traits of personality and factor theory. *American Journal of Psychology, 48,* 673–680.

Hart, B.M., Allen, K.E., Buell, J.S., Harris, F.R., & Wolf, M.M. (1964). Effects of social reinforcement on operant crying. *Journal of Experimental Child Psychology, 1,* 145–153.

Hartley, D. (1749). *Observations on Man. His frame, his duty and his expectations.* London: Johnson.

Hearnshaw, L. (1987). *The shaping of modern psychology: An historical introduction.* London: Routledge & Kegan Paul.

Heather, N. (1976). *Radical perspectives in psychology.* London: Methuen.

Hilgard, E.R. (1986). *Divided consciousness: Multiple controls in human thought and action.* New York: Wiley-Interscience.

Hilgard, E.R., & Bower, G.H. (1981). *Theories of learning* (5th ed.). Englewood Cliffs, NJ: Prentice-Hall.

Hobson, J.A., & McCarley, R.W. (1977). The brain as a dream state generator: An activation-synthesis hypothesis of the dream process. *American Journal of Psychiatry, 121.*

Hockey, G.R.J., Davies, S., & Gray, M.M. (1972). Forgetting as a function of sleep at different times of day. *Quarterly Journal of Experimental Psychology, 24,* 386–393.

Hoffman, A. (1967). Psychomimetic agents. In A. Berger (Ed.), *Drugs affecting the central nervous system, Vol. 2.* New York: Marcel Dekker.

Holt, R.R. (1967). Individuality and generalization in the psychology of personality. In R.L. Lazarus & J.R. Opton (Eds.), *Personality.* Harmondsworth: Penguin.

Hovland, C.I., & Sears, R.R. (1940). Minor studies of aggression: Correlation of lynchings with economic indices. *Journal of Psychology, 9,* 301–310.

Hull, C.L. (1943). *Principles of behaviour.* New York: Appleton-Century-Crofts.

Hume, D. (1739/40). *A treatise of human nature.* London: Noon.

James, W. (1890). *Principles of psychology.* New York: Holt.

Jenkins, J.G., & Dallenbach, K.M. (1924). Obliviscence during sleep and waking. *American Journal of Psychology, 35,* 605–612.

Jensen, A.R. (1969). How much can we boost I.Q. and scholastic achievement? *Harvard Educational Review, 39,* 1–123

Jones, M.B., & Fennell, R.S. (1965). Running performance by two strains of rats. *Quarterly Journal of the Florida Academy of Science, 28,* 289–296.

Jourard, S.M. (1969). The effects of experimenter's self-disclosure on subjects' behaviour. In C.D. Spielberger (Ed.), *Current topics in clinical and community psychology.* New York: Academic Press.

Kelman, H.C. (1972). The rights of the subject in social research: An analysis in terms of relative power and legitimacy. *American Psychologist, 27,* 989–1016.

Koch, S. (1969). Psychology cannot be a coherent science. *Psychology Today, 14,* 64–68.

Kuhn, T.S. (1962). *The structure of scientific revolutions.* Chicago: Chicago University Press.

Kuhn, T.S. (1970). *The structure of scientific revolutions* (2nd ed.). Chicago: Chicago University Press.

Lacey, J.I. (1967). Somatic response patterning and stress: Some revisions of activation theory. In M.H. Appley & R. Trumball (Eds.), *Psychological stress: Issues in research.* New York: Appleton-Century-Crofts

Laird, J.D. (1974). Self-attribution of emotion: The effects of facial expression on the quality of emotional experience. *Journal of Personality and Social Psychology, 29,* 475–486

Latham, G.P., & Yukl, G.A. (1975). Assigned versus participative goal setting with educated and uneducated woods workers. *Journal of Applied Psychology, 60,* 299–302.

Lazarus, Fl.S. (1966). *Psychological stress and the coping process.* New York: McGraw-Hill.

Lazarus, Ii.S. (1982). Thoughts on the relations between emotion and cognition. *American Psychologist, 37,* 1019–1024.

Le Bon, G. (1895). *Psychologie des Foules.* Paris: Alcan.

Lerner, R.M. (1986). *Concepts and theories of human development* (2nd ed.). New York: Random House.

Lick, J. (1975). Expectancy, false galvanic skin response feedback and systematic desensitization in the modification of phobic behaviour. *Journal of Consulting and Clinical Psychology, 43,* 557–567.

Locke, E.A. (1968). Toward a theory of task motivation and incentives. *Organizational Behavior and Human Performance, 3,* 157–189.

Locke, E.A., Shaw, K.N., Saari, L.M., & Latham, G.P. (1981). Goal setting and task performance: 1969–1980. *Psychological Bulletin, 90,* 125–152.

Loftus, E.F. (1979). *Eyewitness testimony.* Cambridge, MA.: Harvard University Press.

Loftus, E.F., & Palmer, J.C. (1974). Reconstruction of automobile destruction: An example of the interaction between language and memory. *Journal of Verbal Learning and Verbal Memory, 13,* 585–489

Lorenz, K.Z. (1935). The companion in the bird's world. *Auk, 54,* 245–273.

Lorenz, K.Z. (1966). *On aggression.* London: Methuen.

Loveless, N.E. (1983). Event-related brain potentials and human performance. In A. Gale & J.A. Edwards (Eds.), *Attention and performance, Vol. 2: Physiological correlates of human behaviour.* London: Academic Press.

Mabbott, J.D. (1954). Free will. In *Encylopaedia Britannica, Vol. 9.* London: Encyclopaedia Britannica Ltd.

Malim, T., Birch, A., & Wadeley, A. (1992). *Perspectives in psychology.* London: Macmillan.

Maranon, G. (1924). Contribution à l'étude de l'action emotive de l'adrenalin. *Revue Français d'Endocrinologie, 2,* 301–325.

Marshall, G.D., & Zimbardo, P.G. (1979). Affective consequences of inadequately explained physiological arousal. *Journal of Personality and Social Psychology, 37,* 970–988.

Maslow, A.H. (1954). *Motivation and personality.* New York: Harper.

Maslow, A.H. (1962). *Toward a psychology of being.* Princeton, NJ: Van Nostrand.

Maslow, A.H. (1968). *Towards a psychology of being.* New York: Van Nostrand.

McCrae, R.R., & Costa, P.T. (1985). Updating Norman's "adequate taxonomy": Intelligence and personality dimensions in natural language and in questionnaires. *Journal of Personality and Social Psychology, 49,* 710–721.

McDougall, W. (1912). *Psychology: The study of behaviour.* London: Williams & Norgate.

McLean, P.D. (1973). *A triune concept of the brain and behaviour.* Toronto: University of Toronto.

Mead, M. (1928). *Coming of age in Samoa.* New York: Morrow.

Meehl, P.E. (1954). *Clinical versus statistical prediction: A theoretical analysis and a review of the evidence.* Minneapolis: University of Minneapolis.

Menges, R.J. (1973). Openness and honesty versus coercion and deception in psychological research. *American Psychologist, 28,* 1030–1034.

Milgram, S. (1974). *Obedience to authority.* London: Harper & Row.

Muller, J. (1833/40). *Handbuch der Physiologie des Menschen.* Coblenz: Holscher.

Murphy, G., & Kovach, J.K. (1972). *Historical introduction to modern psychology.* London: Routledge & Kegan Paul.

Neisser, U. (1978). Memory: What are the important questions? In M.M. Gruneberg, P.F. Morris, & R.N. Sykes (Eds.), *Practical aspects of memory.* London: Academic Press.

Nisbett, R.E., & Wilson, T.D. (1977). Telling more than we can know: Verbal reports on mental processes. *Psychological Review, 84,* 231–259.

Olds, J., & Milner, P. (1954). Positive reinforcement produced by electrical stimulation of septal area and other regions of rat brain. *Journal of Comparative and Physiological Psychology, 47,* 419–427.

Orne, M.T. (1962). On the social psychology of the psychological experiment: With particular reference to demand characteristics and their implications. *American Psychologist, 17,* 776–783.

Petersen, S.E., Fox, P.T., Posner, M.I., Mintun, M., & Raichle, M.E. (1988). Positron emission tomographic studies of the cortical anatomy of single-word processing. *Nature, 331,* 585–589.

Popper, K.R. (1972). *Objective knowledge.* Oxford: Oxford University Press.

Putnam, H. (1973). Reductionism and the nature of psychology. *Cognition, 2,* 131–146.

Rainwater, L., & Yancey, W.L. (1967). *The Moynihan Report and the politics of controversy.* Cambridge, MA: MIT Press.

Reid, T. (1785). *Essays on the intellectual powers of man.* Cambridge: Bartlett.

Rogers, C.R. (1959). A theory of therapy, personality, and interpersonal relationships, as developed in the client-centred framework. In S. Koch (Ed.), *Psychology: A study of a science,* Vol. 3. NY: McGraw-Hill.

Rosenberg, M.J. (1965). When dissonance fails: On eliminating evaluation apprehension from attitude measurement. *Journal of Personality and Social Psychology, 1,* 28–42.

Rosenberg, M.J. (1969). The conditions and consequences of evaluation apprehension. In R. Rosenthal & R. Rosnow (Eds.), *Artifact in Behavioural Research.* London: Academic Press.

Rosenthal, R. (1967). *Experimenter effects in behavioural research.* New York: Appleton-Century-Crofts.

Schachter, S., & Singer, J.E. (1962). Cognitive, social and physiological determinants of an emotional state. *Psychological Review, 69,* 379–399.

Schachter, S., & Wheeler, L. (1962). Epinephrine, chlorpromazine and amusement. *Journal of Abnormal and Social Psychology, 65,* 121–128.

Seligman, M.E.P. (1970). On the generality of the laws of learning. *Psychological Review, 77,* 406–418.

Shallice, T. (1982). Specific impairments of planning. *Philosophical Transactions of the Royal Society of London, B298,* 199–209

Shallice, T., & Warrington, E.K. (1970). Independent functioning of verbal memory stores: A neuropsychological study. *Quarterly Journal of Experimental Psychology, 22,* 261–273.

Sigall, H., Aronson, E., & Van Hoose, T. (1970). The co-operative subject: Myth or reality? *Journal of Experimental Social Psychology, 6,* 1–10.

Silverman, I. (1977). *The human subject in the psychological laboratory.* Oxford: Pergamon.

Silverman, I., Shulman, A.D., & Wiesenthal, D. (1970). Effects of deceiving and debriefing psychological subjects on performance in later experiments. *Journal of Personality and Social Psychology, 21,* 219–227.

Silverstein, C. (1972). *Behaviour modification and the gay community.* Paper presented at the annual convention of the Association for Advancement of Behaviour Therapy, New York.

Simmons, J.V. (1981). *Project Sea Hunt: A report on prototype development and tests.* Technical Report, No. 746. San Diego: Naval Ocean System Center.

Skinner, B.F. (1948). *Walden Two.* New York: Macmillan.

Skinner, B.F. (1953). *Science and human behaviour.* New York: Macmillan.

Skinner, B.F. (1957). *Verbal behaviour.* New York: Appleton-Century-Crofts.

Skinner, B.F. (1966). Operant behaviour. In W.K. Honig (Ed.), *Operant behaviour: Areas of research and application.* New York: Appleton-Century-Crofts.

Skinner, B.F. (1971). *Beyond freedom and dignity.* New York: Knopf.

Skinner, B.F. (1980). *The shaping of a behaviourist.* Oxford: Holdan Books.

Slater, A. (1989). Visual memory and perception in early infancy. In A. Slater & G. Bremner (Eds.), *Infant Development.* Hove: Lawrence Erlbaum Associates Ltd.

Slater, A., & Morison, V. (1985). Shape constancy and slant perception at birth. *Perception, 14,* 337-344.

Smith, P.K. (1983). Human sociobiology. In J. Nicholson & B. Foss (Eds.), *Psychology Survey, No. 4.* Leicester: British Psychological Society.

Smith, S.M., Brown, H. O., Toman, J.E.P., & Goodman, L.S. (1947). Lack of cerebral effects of D-tubocurarine. *Anaesthesiology, 8,* 1–14.

Spearman, C. (1927). *The abilities of Man.* London: Macmillan.

Taylor, A., Sluckin, W., Davies, D.R., Reason, J.T., Thomson, R., & Colman, A.M. (1982). *Introducing psychology* (2nd ed.). Harmondsworth: Penguin.

Tellegen, A. (1985). Structures of mood and personality and their relevance to assessing anxiety, with an emphasis on self-report. In A.H. Tuma & J. Maser (Eds.), *Anxiety and the anxiety disorders.* Hillsdale: Lawrence Erlbaum Associates.

Terrace, H.S. (1979). *Nim.* New York: Alfred Knopf.

Thomson, R. (1968). *The Pelican history of psychology.* Harmondsworth: Penguin.

Thorndike, E.L. (1898). Animal intelligence: An experimental study of the associative processes in animals. *The Psychological Review Monograph Supplements, 2,* No. 4 (Whole No. 8).

Tulving, E. (1989). Memory: Performance, knowledge, and experience. *European Journal of Cognitive Psychology, 1,* 3–26.

Tulving, E., Schacter, D.L., & Stark, H.A. (1982). Priming effects in word-fragment completion are independent of recognition memory. *Journal of Experimental Psychology: Learning, Memory, and Cognition, 8,* 336–342.

Valentine, E.R. (1992). *Conceptual issues in psychology* (2nd ed.). London: Routledge.

Wachtel, P.L. (1973). Psychodynamics, behaviour therapy and the implacable experimenter: An inquiry into the consistency of personality. *Journal of Abnormal Psychology, 82,* 324–334.

Watson, J.B. (1913). Psychology as the behaviourist views it. *Psychological Review, 20,* 158–177.

Watson, J.B. (1924). *Psychology from the standpoint of a behaviourist.* (2nd ed.). Philadelphia: Lippincott.

Weiskrantz, L. (1986). *Blindsight: A case study and implications.* Oxford: Oxford University Press.

Wernicke, C. (1874). *Der Aphasische*

*Symptomencomplex.*Breslau: Cohn & Weigart.

Wilson, E.O. (1975). *Sociobiology: The New Synthesis*. Harvard: Harvard Univ. Press.

Wittgenstein, L. (1958). *Philosophical investigations*. New York: Macmillan.

Wundt, W. (1873). *Grundzuge der Physiologischer Psychologie*. Leipzig: W. Engelmann.

Zajonc, R.B. (1980). Feeling and thinking: Preferences need no inferences. *American Psychologist, 35*, 151–175.

Zajonc, R.B. (1984). On the primacy of affect. *American Psychologist, 39*, 117–123.

# Glossary

**Ability:** in Locke's goal theory, the necessary skills and knowledge to attain the goal

**Abnormal psychology:** the study of patients suffering from a wide variety of clinical conditions

**Acquired motives:** see Secondary motives

**Activity raising:** part of cognitive therapy (q.v.) in which depressed patients are rewarded for increased involvement in activities

**Amnesis barriers:** separations between parts of the body's system produced by hypnosis according to Hilgard

**Analytical introspection:** verbal reports focusing on specific parts of one's experience; see also Phenomenology

**Animal experiments:** studies conducted on other species

**Appeasement rituals:** forms of behaviour designed to prevent aggressive behaviour by others

**Archive material:** information gathered by governments and other organisations which can be of value to social psychologists

**Associationism:** the view of Aristotle and others that thinking is based on the association of ideas

**Autobiographical memory:** see Episodic memory

**Automatic processes:** rapid processes resulting from extensive practice and generally not associated with conscious awareness

**Aversion therapy:** a form of treatment in which the undesired behaviour is followed rapidly by an unpleasant stimulus (e.g., electric shock)

**Basic motives:** see Primary motives

**Behavioural component of emotion:** the pattern of behaviour associated with a given emotional state

**Behavioural observations:** measures of observable behaviour

**Behavioural phenotype:** general and habitual characteristics of behaviour; see also Genotype

**Behaviour modification:** the application of operant conditioning (q.v.) to behavioural problems and mental disorders

**Behaviour therapy:** an approach to the treatment of mental disorders based on conditioning principles

**Behaviourism:** an American school of psychology in which there was an emphasis on measuring behaviour and on conditioning principles

**Behaviourists:** psychologists who advocate behaviourism (q.v.)

**Biological approach:** the approach to psychology pioneered by Darwin, with an emphasis on comparative psychology (q.v.), heredity, and individual differences

**Blind sight:** a phenomenon in which patients can make accurate decisions about objects in the visual field in spite of lacking conscious awareness of these objects

**Broca's speech area:** an area of the brain involved in speech but not in language comprehension; see also Wernicke's area

**Cannon-Bard theory:** a theory of emotion in which the role of the thalamus is emphasised

**Cause and effect:** as applied to the experimental method, the notion that changes in the independent variable (q.v.) may cause changes in the dependent variable (q.v.)

**Client-centred therapy:** a form of treatment introduced by Carl Rogers, in which the therapist (or facilitator) provides the client with a very supportive environment

**Clinical method:** predicting clinical outcomes (e.g., recovery of psychiatric patients) by the use of subjective judgement; see also Statistical method

**Cognitive appraisal:** the assessment of the emotional significance of a situation which according to Lazarus precedes any emotional state

**Cognitive component of emotion:** that aspect of emotion depending on analysis of the situation

**Cognitive labelling theory:** a theory of emotion proposed by Schachter and Singer, according to which emotional experience depends on the labelling of physiological arousal

**Cognitive neuropsychology:** the study of cognitive functioning in brain-damaged patients

**Cognitive psychology:** the study of processes such as attention, perception, learning, memory, and thinking

**Cognitive science:** an approach to cognitive psychology (q.v.) in which computer programs are often used to mimic human cognition processes and behaviour

**Cognitive therapy:** a form of treatment based largely on changing the patient's beliefs and interpretations

**Comparative psychology:** an approach to psychology involving comparisons across species

**Computer analogy:** the view that human cognition can be compared to the functioning of computers

**Concordance:** agreement between different components of an emotion which is more widely expected than obtained

**Confidentiality:** the requirement that information provided by individual subjects in research is not available to other people

**Confounding variables:** variables which are mistakenly manipulated along with the independent variable (q.v.) and which prevent findings from being interpreted

**Conscious experience:** experience which is constantly changing, combines information across modalities, and reflects the products of thought processes

**Control:** one of the goals of science, along with prediction (q.v.) and understanding (q.v.)

**Correlational designs:** designs in which there is no manipulation of the situation, and in which the association between two (or more) responses is assessed

**Cyclic motives:** motives (e.g., need to sleep) which increase and decrease in a fairly predictable fashion; see also Non-cyclic motives

**Debriefing:** providing full information about an experiment to someone who has participated in it

**Demand characteristics:** cues used by subjects in an experiment to try to work out what the experiment is about

**Dependent variable:** the aspect of subjects' behaviour measured in an experiment; see also Independent variable

**Determinism:** the view that all behaviour has some definite cause or causes; see also Free will

**Developmental psychology:** an approach to psychology focusing on psychological changes during childhood; often extended to adulthood and old age

**Double aspect theory:** a view proposed by Spinoza, according to which mental and physical processes reflect the same underlying reality

**Double blind:** a precaution in experimental research, in which neither the experimenter in the laboratory nor the person analysing the data knows what is being tested

**Down's syndrome:** a hereditary condition in which there is moderate mental retardation

**Drive-reduction theory:** a theory proposed by Hull and others, in which it is assumed that it is rewarding to reduce drives (q.v.)

**Drives:** motivational forces which are more psychological and less physiological than needs (q.v.)

**Ecological validity:** the extent to which the findings of laboratory studies are applicable to everyday settings

**ECT:** see Electroconvulsive shock treatment

**EEG:** see Electroencephalogram

**Ego:** the conscious, rational mind; one of the three main parts of the mind in Freud's theory

**Electroconvulsive shock treatment:** administration of strong electric current from electrodes attached to the forehead; used to treat severe depression; abbreviated as ECT

**Electroencephalogram:** assessment of brain-wave activity in different parts of the brain; abbreviated as EEG

**Emotion:** a state involving bodily changes, strong feelings, and impulses towards certain kinds of behaviour

**Empiricism:** the notion that science should be based on objective measurement

**Empiricists:** those who argue that behaviour is determined by environmental factors and by learning; see also Nativists

**Episodic memory:** the part of long-term memory concerned with personal events or episodes of an autobiographical nature

**Equipotentiality:** the view that essentially any response can be conditioned to any stimulus

**ERP:** see evoked response potential

**Ethical committees:** groups which decide whether proposed experiments would infringe the rights and dignity of subjects

**Evaluation apprehension:** the desire of subjects to be positively evaluated by the experimenter

**Evoked response potential:** averaging of brain-wave activity across several presentations of a stimulus to identify the activity produced by that stimulus, abbreviated as ERP

**Existentialism:** a philosophical approach which emphasises personal responsibility, free will (q.v.), and personal growth

**Experiential component of emotion:** the consciously experienced feelings associated with an emotional state

**Experimental cognitive psychology:** an approach to human cognition generally involving laboratory experiments

**Experimental hypothesis:** the experimenter's prediction as to what will happen in a given experiment

**Experimental method:** the observation of behaviour under controlled conditions; see also Introspection

**Experimenter bias:** influence of an experimenter's expectations on the results obtained

**Expressive component of emotion:** facial expression, bodily posture, and other non-verbal behaviour reflecting emotion

**External validity:** the validity of research findings outside the research situation

**Externally aroused:** as applied to motives, those which are triggered off by external stimuli; see also Internally aroused

**Extrinsic motivation:** motivation which depends on external incentives and rewards; see also Intrinsic motivation

**Factor analysis:** a statistical method for identifying the underlying components of intelligence and personality from test data

**Feedback:** in Locke's goal theory, information about the progress towards a goal provided to the individual

**Field experiments:** the application of the experimental method (q.v.) in naturalistic settings

**Field observations:** observations made by an experimenter in real-life settings with no attempt being made to control the situation

**Fixates:** in Freudian theory, the child fixates or spends unduly long in a given stage of development if severe problems are encountered; see also Regress

**Free will:** the notion that we are free to make decisions; this view contrasts with determinism (q.v.)

**Functionalist:** a school of psychology founded by John Dewey, involving an emphasis on the functional value of behaviour

**Generalisations:** general statements based on experimental findings and observations, and providing the basis for theories

**Genotype:** an individual's genetic potential; see also Phenotype

**Genotypic differences:** individual differences in the genotype (q.v.), which play a role in determining individual differences in behaviour

**Gestalt:** a German school of psychology in which the focus was on studying perception and problem solving through the use of Phenomenology (q.v.)

**Goal commitment:** in Locke's goal theory, the extent to which the individual accepts the goal which has been set

**Goal theory:** a cognitive theory of motivation proposed by Locke, according to which performance depends on goal setting and goal commitment (q.v.)

**Graded task assignment:** a part of cognitive therapy (q.v.) in which depressed patients are given specific tasks to perform

**Habituation:** as applied to visual perception in infants, the finding that they spend less and less time looking at a repeated stimulus

**Hierarchy of needs:** in Maslow's theory, physiological needs are at the bottom of the need hierarchy, and the need for self-actualisation is at the top

**Hierarchy of motives:** see Hierarchy of needs

**Homeostasis:** the processes maintaining a reasonably constant internal environment

**Homeostatic drive theory:** the view that lack of internal balance or homeostasis (q.v.) produces motivation to correct the imbalance

**Homogeneous groups:** groups of comparable subjects; often difficult to form with brain-damaged patients

**Human sociobiology:** approach in which biology is applied to social behaviour

**Humanistic psychology:** an approach derived from existentialism (q.v.) which emphasises the self-concept, the value of conscious experience, and our attempts to realise our potential

**Hypnosis:** a state of heightened suggestibility which may or may not represent an altered state of consciousness

**Hypothalamus:** a part of the brain which, when damaged, can have substantial effects on hunger

**Hypotheses:** the testable predictions generated by a theory

**Id:** in Freudian theory, that part of the mind which is the repository of the sexual instinct; see also Ego and Superego

**Idiographic approach:** an approach to psychology which emphasises the uniqueness of each individual and the importance of studying individuals

**Implacable experimenter:** the situation in most experimental research, in which the experimenter's behaviour is uninfluenced by the subject's behaviour

**Imprinting:** a strong tendency for the young of some species (e.g., geese) to follow the first moving object they encounter

**Incongruence:** in Rogers' client-centred therapy (q.v.), a large discrepancy between the self-concept and the ideal self

**Independent variable:** an aspect of the experimental situation which is manipulated by the experimenter

**Individual differences:** an approach to psychology in which differences among individuals in intelligence and personality are emphasised

**Inner-biological level:** physiological influences on the unborn child

**Inner-psychological level:** mother's psychological influences on the unborn child

**Insight:** in Freudian theory, access to and understanding of emotional memories emerging from the unconscious; the goal of therapy

**Instinctive drift:** the characteristic ways of behaving of each species, only partially alterable by training

**Instincts:** innate capacities or patterns of responding

**Internal validity:** the validity of an experiment in terms of the context in which it is carried out; see also External validity

**Internally aroused:** as applied to motives, those (e.g., food; drink) which depend mainly on internal factors; see also Externally aroused

**Interviews:** a method for investigating people's attitudes and behaviour; often unduly influenced by the interviewer's behaviour

**Intrinsic motivation:** motivation for which the rewards are internal (e.g., feelings of competence) rather than external (e.g., money); see also Extrinsic motivation

**Introspection:** examination and observation of one's own mental processes

**James-Lange theory:** a theory of emotion in which it is assumed that the experience of emotion depends on feedback from bodily changes

**Latent content:** in Freud's theory of dreams, the real meaning of a dream, in contrast to the manifest content (q.v.)

**Law of parsimony:** a scientific theory should make as few assumptions as possible

**Laws of association:** the notion, going back to Plato and Aristotle, that thinking involves an association of ideas (i.e., one idea will trigger off another similar idea)

**Learned motives:** see Secondary motives

**Lie scale:** items incorporated into personality tests in which the honest answer is unlikely to be the socially desirable one; used to detect dishonesty

**Limbic system:** a part of the brain involved in emotion

**Logos:** the Greek word for study; the word psychology derives from psyche (q.v.) and logos

**Longitudinal study:** an investigation which is carried out over a relatively long period of time

**Manifest content:** in Freud's theory of dreams, the apparent meaning of a dream rather than its actual meaning; see also Latent content

**Maternal deprivation:** term popularised by Bowlby refering to absence of a continuous loving bond between mother and child

**Motivation:** the process that arouses, maintains, and regulates behaviour

**Nancy school:** French scientists who used the power of suggestion to cure mental illness (e.g., hysteria)

**Nativists:** those who emphasise the role of nature (q.v.) or heredity in determining behaviour; see also Empiricists

**Nature:** see Nature-nurture controversy

**Nature and nurture:** see Nature-nurture controversy

**Nature-nurture controversy:** disagreements over the relative importance of nature or heredity and nurture or environment in determining behaviour

**Nature of science:** scientists make observations which are partially determined by theory, and propose hypotheses which are falsifiable

**Needs:** motives which depend largely on physiology; see also Drives

**Negative affect:** within Tellegen's theory, one of two major independent dimensions of mood; see also Positive affect

**Neo-dissociation theory:** a theory proposed by Hilgard to account for hypnotic phenomena; it is based on the notion that one part of the body is separated off from other parts in hypnosis; see also Amnesic barriers

**Neocortex:** the part of the brain concerned with language and other higher-level cognitive functions

**Neurosis:** a broad category of mental illness in which there is no loss of contact with reality (e.g., the anxiety disorders); see also Psychosis

**Nomothetic approach:** an approach to psychology based on the attempt to establish general laws of behaviour; see also Idiographic approach

**Non-cyclic motives:** motives which do not increase and decrease in fairly predictable ways over time; usually externally aroused (q.v.)

**Non-representative samples:** the use of groups of subjects in research which do not reflect a wider population

**Normal mode of science:** a period of time during which most scientists accept a dominant general theoretical orientation; see also Revolutionary mode of science

**Nurture:** see Nature-nurture controversy

**Objective data gathering:** The view that scientists collect data in an objective or unbiased fashion

**Observational methods:** an approach to research in which the emphasis is on detailed observations of behaviour

**Operant conditioning:** a form of learning in which behaviour can be controlled by providing reward or reinforcement appropriately

**Operational definitions:** definitions which indicate how concepts are to be measured

**Paleocortex:** see Limbic system

**Paradigm:** in Kuhn's theory, a general theoretical orientation which is accepted by most scientists in a given discipline

**Parallel distributed processing:** a class of models in cognitive science (q.v.), in which computer programs perform several different operations at the same time

**Peak experiences:** heightened experiences associated with feelings of euphoria and wonder; term introduced by Maslow

**Personal space:** an area around each individual which he or she does not like most other people to invade

**PET:** see Positron emission tomography

**Phenomenology:** an approach focusing on the reporting of pure experience

**Phenotype:** observable characteristics of an individual (e.g., eye colour); see also Genotype

**Philosophy:** a discipline concerned with the search for wisdom and knowledge

**Physical-environmental level:** effects on children of aspects of the physical environment (e.g., lead in the atmosphere)

**Physiological component of emotion:** that aspect of emotion concerned with bodily changes (e.g., activity in the autonomic nervous system)

**Physiological psychology:** research (mainly on other species) in which the effects of some physiological manipulation on behaviour are observed

**Positive affect:** in Tellegen's theory, one of two major independent dimensions of mood; see also Negative affect

**Positron emission tomography:** a technique designed to assess activity in different parts of the brain; it makes use of a PET scanner

**Post-traumatic stress disorder:** an anxiety disorder produced by some extremely stressful event (e.g., rape)

**Pre-programmed:** behaviour which depends on heredity rather than on learning processes

**Prediction:** the ability to predict or anticipate the outcomes of experiments is one of the main goals of science

**Preparedness:** the notion that each species finds some forms of learning more 'natural' and easier than others; a term introduced by Seligman

**Primary appraisal:** in Lazarus' theory of emotion, the process involved in deciding whether a situation is positive, stressful, or irrelevant to well-being

**Primary motives:** basic needs (e.g., for food) found throughout the members of any given species

**Priming effects:** facilitating effects on performance of previously presented stimuli

**Propensities:** a term used by McDougall to refer to basic motives such as those for food-seeking, sex, and rest

**Psyche:** the Greek word meaning mind or soul; the word psychology derives from this word and from logos (q.v.)

**Psychoanalysis:** Freud' set of theories about human behaviour, and the form of treatment for mental disorders which he devised

**Psychometrics:** the design and use of psychological tests (e.g., of intelligence and personality)

**Psychophysical parallelism:** the view put forward by Leibnitz, according to which mental and physical events occur simultaneously but do not interact with each other

**Psychophysiology:** an approach in which physiological measures (e.g., heart rate; respiratory rate) are taken in order to increase our understanding of behaviour; see also Physiological psychology

**Psychophysiological data:** physiological measures obtained by scientists in psychophysiology (q.v.)

**Psychosis:** a form of mental disorder in which there is partial or complete loss of contact with reality; examples are manic-depressive psychosis and schizophrenia

**Psychotherapy:** an approach to treatment originated by Freud and involving changes to cognitive processes and structures

**Q-sort method:** as used by Carl Rogers, a technique for assessing the self-concept and the ideal self

**Questionnaires:** self-report assessments of individual characteristics (e.g., intelligence; personality)

**Reductionists:** those who believe that psychology can ultimately be reduced to more basic scientific disciplines (e.g., physiology)

**Regional cerebral blood flow:** a method for assessing activity in different parts of the brain based on radioactivity levels

**Regress:** in Freudian theory, the tendency of mentally disordered individuals to return to earlier stages of development

**Replicability:** a desirable feature of research, in which the findings of an experiment can be repeated by others

**Replication:** see Replicability

**Repression:** in Freudian theory, the process by which traumatic memories are forced into the unconscious; motivated forgetting

**Reptile brain:** those parts of the brain stem and lower part of the brain concerned with basic functions (e.g., breathing)

**Response specificity:** a term in psychophysiology meaning that individuals differ in terms of their most and least responsive psychophysiological measures

**Revolutionary mode of science:** a period of time during which a previously accepted general theoretical orientation is overthrown; see also Normal mode of science

**Rewards:** in Locke's goal theory, the benefits derived from goal attainment

**Right to withdraw:** the basic right of subjects in experiments to stop their involvement at any point

**Ritualisation:** expression of aggression in a stereotyped fashion; see also Appeasement rituals

**Role-playing:** as applied to experiments, studies in which subjects are asked to imagine how they would behave in certain situations

**Samples:** Groups selected from some larger population for experimental purposes

**Secondary appraisal:** in Lazarus' theory of emotion, the stage at which the individual considers his or her resources for coping with a situation

**Secondary motives:** learned motives which are based on Primary motives (q.v.)

**Self-report data:** questionnaires, interviews, and other forms of information provided by individuals

**Semantic memory:** a major part of long-term memory, concerned with our knowledge of facts and meanings

**Septo-hippocampal system:** a part of the brain of central importance in anxiety

**Single-case studies:** research in which the focus is on individual subjects; most common in clinical studies and studies of brain-damaged patients

**Sleep:** a state of physiological rest which can be divided into five different stages (e.g., rapid eye movement or REM sleep)

**Social control:** the application of psychological principles to control the members of society

**Social desirability bias:** the tendency on questionnaires to provide the socially desirable rather than the honest answer; see also Lie scale

**Social facilitation:** Allport's proposed explanation of the finding that individuals often work better in social situations

**Social identity theory:** a theory in social psychology in which the broad social context is emphasised

**Social psychology:** an approach to psychology focusing on our relationships to other people and to society

**Social representation theory:** a largely European theory in social psychology, with an emphasis on the context provided by society

**Sociocultural level:** influences of educational, recreational, and other practices on a child's development

**Soft determinism:** the notion that behaviour is determined, but that the situational constraints on behaviour may be strong or weak; see also Determinism

**Somatic therapy:** clinical treatment based on bodily manipulations (e.g., drug administration)

**Statistical method:** predicting clinical outcomes (e.g., criminals' relapse into crime) using standardised tests; see Clinical methods

**Sternberg paradigm:** method for measuring retrieval speed from short-term memory

**Stimulus-response associations:** according to the behaviourists (q.v.), the simple units out of which complex behaviour emerges

**Superego:** in Freudian theory, the part of the mind concerned with moral issues

**Support:** in Locke's goal theory, the encouragement provided by management to individual workers systematic desensitisation: a form of behaviour therapy (q.v.), in which phobias are reduced by associating phobic stimuli (e.g., snakes) with physical relaxation responses

**Token economy:** a form of treatment used with clinical patients and criminals based on providing reward; see Operant Conditioning

**Trait anxiety:** a personality dimension involving a predisposition to experience anxiety

**Treatment:** therapy for mentally disordered patients, and including Behaviour therapy (q.v.), Cognitive therapy (q.v.), and Somatic therapy (q.v.)

**Tropisms:** simple responses to stimulation exhibited by plants

**Understanding:** one of the main goals of science

**Unlearned motives:** see Primary motives

**Variables:** in correlational designs, the response measures obtained from the subjects

**Voluntary informed consent:** the requirement for ethical research that potential subjects agree to participate after being informed of what they will be asked to do

**Vulnerable participants:** subjects in experiments who are relatively powerless compared to the experimenter

**Wernicke's area:** the part of the brain involved in language comprehension, but not speech production; the opposite to Broca's area (q.v.)

**Wish fulfilment:** in Freud's theory of dreams, the notion that all dreams represent the satisfaction of desires (often in a disguised form)

**Withdrawal symptoms:** problems which occur when patients finish a course of drug treatment

**Work psychology:** the study of Occupational performance

# Author index

# Subject index

Gestalt school, 10, 47, 57, 68
goal theory, 95–6, *see also* motivation

habituation, 46
happiness, and age, 131, 137–8
Hartley, David, 11
Helmholtz, Hermann von, 34, 35, 57
heredity, 28, 38–9, 68, 71, *see also* nature vs. nurture
homeostatic drive theory, 91–2
homogeneity of subject groups, 133–4
homosexuality, 132–3, 149–50
human experimental subjects, 143–9
human sociobiology, 29–30
humanistic psychology, 46–51, 57, 63–4, 113–15
Hume, David, 11
hunger, 92
hypnosis, 17–18, 19, 79–80
hypothalamus, 92, 99
hypotheses, 108, 116

id, 7, 18
idiographic approach, 72–4, 75–6, 115–16, *see also* single-case studies
"implacable" experimenter, 126
imprinting, 31
independent variables, 116
individual differences, 38–40, 57, 72–5, *see also* nature vs. nurture
insight, 19, 112
instinctive drift, 157
instincts (innate responses), 31
instincts (motives), 89

intelligence, 38–9, 40, 69, 154
internal validity of research, 118–19, 128
interviewing, 135–7, 138
intrinsic motivation, theory of, 94–5
introspection, 1, 47, 83–5

James, William, 66, 67, 77–8
James-Lange theory of emotion, 98–9

labelling, cognitive, 101–2
laboratory experiments, 118–21
language
    acquisition of, 63
    and animals, 33–4
learning, 22, 25
    animal studies, 127, 155, 157
    and reinforcement, 25, 110, 155–7
Leibnitz, Gottfried, 9–10
lie scale, 136
Loeb, Jacques, 20–1
longitudinal studies, 72
Lorenz, Konrad, 31–2
LSD, 79

Maslow, Abraham H., 47, 48–9, 91, 96, 115, 152
maternal deprivation, 45
memory
    episodic and semantic, 36–7
    and hypnosis, 80
    priming effects, 78–9
    research on, 117, 119–21, 133
"mental health", 6
mental illness
    drug treatment, 26, 27
    electroconvulsive shock treatment (ECT), 25

ethics in therapy, 149–50
    history, 17–18
    and psychoanalysis, 19–20, 25
    psychotherapy, 23–5
Mesmer, Franz, 17
methodology, research, 2, 12, 22–3, 107–40, *see also* ethics
    data collection, 135–9
    experimental method, 2, 12, 22–3, 116–31
    idiographic *vs.* nomothetic approaches, 72–6
    observation, 30, 31
    psychology and science, 111–16
    and science, 107–11
    single-case studies, 131–4
    social psychology, 41–2
Milgram, Stanley, shock experiment, 5, 143–4, 146–7
mind, *see also* consciousness; unconscious
    and body, 6–7, 9–10, 34–5
    study of, 1–3, 9
mood, 97, 104, *see also* emotion
morality, absolute and relative, 152–3
motivation, 12, 48–9, 57, 88–97
    classification of, 90–1
    definition of, 88–9
    theories of, 91–6
Muller, Johannes, 34–5, 57

Nancy school, 17
nativism, 68
nature *vs.* nurture, 12, 68–71
    behaviourism, 22
    deprivation, 45
    intelligence, 38–9
needs, 48–9, 51, 91, 94, 96, *see also* motivation

neo-dissociation theory, 80
neurology, 53
neurosis, 19–20, 24, 112
nomothetic approach, 72, 74–6, 115–16

objectivity, 107, 110–11
observations, 30, 107–8, 129–30
operant conditioning, 155–7
operational definitions, 111

pain, 80
paradigms, 108–9, 116
parallel distributed processing, 54
paranoia, 132–3
parsimony, law of, 111, 112
Pavlov, Ivan Petrovich, 23, 35, 57
peak experiences, 49, 115
perception, 35
personal space, 128
personality, 40, 73–4
phenomenology, 47, 50–1
phenotype, 68–9
phenylketonuria, 71
phobia, 26
physiological psychology, 34–8, 57
physiology, 57, 62
Piaget, Jean, 44, 54, 57
pineal gland, 9
Plato, 6–7, 8
Popper, Karl, 107–8, 110
populations, 126–7
positron emission tomography (PET), 37
post-traumatic stress disorder, 109
power, and social research, 5, 143–4, 146–7
prediction, 66, 109–10
preparedness, 157
"pre-programming", 32

priming, 78–9
propensities, 89
psyche, 1, 7
psychiatry, 1
psychoanalysis, 18–20, 25, 83, 111–13
psychology
   abnormal, 24–7
   behaviourist approach, 20–4, 113
   biological approach, 27–30
   cognitive, 52–6
   and common sense, 3–5
   comparative, 30–4
   definition of, 1–3, 15–16
   development of, 5–11, 16, 57
   developmental, 43–6
   humanistic, 46–51, 113–15
   idiographic vs. nomothetic approaches, 72–6, 115–16
   individual differences, 38–40
   and other disciplines, 11–12, 15, 57, 61–2
   psychoanalytic approach, 17–20, 111–13
   psychophysiological approach, 34–8
   as science, 61–2, 72, 115–16
   social, 40–3
psychometrics, 39–40, 57
psychopharmacology, 57, see also drugs
psychophysical parallelism, 9–10
psychophysiology, 34–8, 57
psychosis, 19
psychotherapy, 23–5, 49–50, 57
   and ethics, 149–50, 156–7

Q-sort method, 114
questionnaires, 135–7, 138

race, 29, 69–70
random sampling, 139
rapid eye movement (REM) sleep, 81, 82
reductionism, 61–4
regional cerebral blood flow, 36
reinforcement, 110, 155–7
relative morality, 152–3
replicability of experimental results, 117
representativeness of experiments, 126–7, 138–9
repression, 19
research, 7
   ethics (q.v.), 13, 142–59
   methodology (q.v.), 12, 107–40
ritualisation, 32
Rogers, Carl, 47, 49–50, 66–7, 114, 152
role-playing experiments, 145
Ryle, Gilbert, 10

samples, 126–7, 138–9
schizophrenia, 64
science, 107–9, see also research
   and determinism, 65–6, 110
   goals of, 109–10
   and idiographic vs. nomothetic approach, 72–6, 115–16
   normal and revolutionary modes of, 108–9
   Plato and Aristotle, 6–7
   psychology as, 61–2, 72, 115–16
   scientific assumptions, 110–11
self-actualisation, 48–9, 51, 63, 115, 152
self-concept, 49–50, 63, 114

self-report, 135–7, 138
semantic memory, 36–7
single-case studies, 131–4
Skinner, B.F., 63, 66, 155–6, 157
sleep, 80–3
social control, 142, 154–8
social desirability bias, 135–6
social psychology, 40–3, 57
sociology, 57, 62
Socrates, 6
"soft" determinism, 66
somatic therapy, 26
soul, 6–7, 9
Spinoza, Baruch, 10
statistics
  factor analysis, 39–40
  statistical method, 75
Sternberg paradigm, 119–20

stimulus-response associations, 21, 22, 113
stream of thought, 11
subjects, experimental, 126–7, *see also* animal studies
  homogeneity of samples, 133–4
  rights of, 143–9
suggestion, power of, 17, 80
superego, 7, 18
survey methods, 137–9
systematic desensitisation, 26

Tellegen's theory of emotion, 104
testing, psychological, 38–40
thalamus, 99–100
theories, 7, 108
Thorndike, Edward L., 21

token economy, 24–5, 156
tropisms, 20–1
twin studies, 39

unconscious mind, 3, 9, 18, 78
understanding, 66, 109, 110

validity of research, 118–19, 128
variables, 116–17, 130–1

Watson, John B., 21–2, 23, 57, 113
Wernicke, Carl, 53, 57
will *see* free will
wish fulfilment, 83
work psychology, 95–6